Constant Leke

Rich in Mercy: Experiencing and Practicing God's Mercy

Constant Leke

Rich in Mercy: Experiencing and Practicing God's Mercy

Blessed Hope Publishing

Imprint
Any brand names and product names mentioned in this book are subject to trademark, brand or patent protection and are trademarks or registered trademarks of their respective holders. The use of brand names, product names, common names, trade names, product descriptions etc. even without a particular marking in this work is in no way to be construed to mean that such names may be regarded as unrestricted in respect of trademark and brand protection legislation and could thus be used by anyone.

Cover image: www.ingimage.com

Publisher:
Blessed Hope Publishing
is a trademark of
Dodo Books Indian Ocean Ltd. and OmniScriptum S.R.L publishing group

120 High Road, East Finchley, London, N2 9ED, United Kingdom
Str. Armeneasca 28/1, office 1, Chisinau MD-2012, Republic of Moldova, Europe
Printed at: see last page
ISBN: 978-620-4-18820-1

RICH IN MERCY: EXPERIENCING AND PRACTICING THE MERCY OF GOD

Rev. Fr. Dr. Constant Leke
"Restorare Omnia in Christo"
To Restore All Things In Christ
(Eph. 1:10)

Scripture quotations are from the Jerusalem Bible popular edition with Abridged Introduction and Notes (London, Darton, Longman & Todd.
Excerpts from the English translation of the Catechism of the Catholic Church- Libreria Editrice Vaticana.
Excerpt from Lumen Gentium, Redemptoris Mater, Marialis Cultis, and other Vatican documents c Libreria Editrice Vaticana.

Cover art:

EXPLANATION OF THE MERCY LOGO AND MOTTO

The motto *Merciful Like the Father* (taken from the Gospel of Luke, 6:36) serves as an invitation to follow the merciful example of the Father who asks us not to judge or condemn but to forgive and to give love and forgiveness without measure (cf. Lk 6:37-38). The logo – the work of Jesuit Father Marko I. Rupnik – presents a small *summa theologiae* of the theme of mercy. In fact, it represents an image quite important to the early Church: that of the Son having taken upon his shoulders the lost soul demonstrating that it is the love of Christ that brings to completion the mystery of his incarnation culminating in redemption. The logo has been designed in such a way so as to express the profound way in which the Good Shepherd touches the flesh of humanity and does so with a love with the power to change one's life. One particular feature worthy of note is that while the Good Shepherd, in his great mercy, takes humanity upon himself, his eyes are merged with those of man. Christ sees with the eyes of Adam, and Adam with the eyes of Christ. Every person discovers in Christ, the new Adam, one's own humanity and the future that lies ahead, contemplating, in his gaze, the love of the Father.

The scene is captured within the so called *mandorla* (the shape of an almond), a figure quite important in early and medieval iconography, for it calls to mind the two natures of Christ, divine and human. The three concentric ovals, with colors progressively lighter as we move outward, suggest the movement of Christ who carries humanity out of the night of sin and death. Conversely, the depth of the darker color suggests the impenetrability of the love of the Father who forgives all.

5

CONTENTS

INSTANCES OF GOD'S MERCY

CHAPTER FIVE..32
APPLICATION OF GOD'S MERCY

CHAPTER SIX...35
CONDITIONS FOR RECEIVING GOD'S MERCY

CHAPTER SEVEN..38
CHRISTIAN MERCY

GENERAL INTRODUCTION

*"I was sinking deep in sin, far from the peaceful shore,
very deeply stained within, sinking to rise no more.
But the Master of the sea heard my despairing cry,
from the waters lifted me, now safe am I." (James Rowe)*

We want to live in the light of the Word of the Lord: "Be merciful, even as your Father is merciful" (cf. Lk 6:36)....

Grace has been defined as "receiving what we don't deserve." Mercy has been defined as "not receiving what we do deserve." I hear children all of the time saying, "That's not fair!" Many times, when life hands us a bad twist we say the same thing, "God, that's just not fair!" Fair would be an eternity without God, and us paying the price for our own sin. That would be impossible, but it would be fair. Anything outside of that is God's mercy.

We live in a world today that needs to see mercy in living color. People who have blown it sexually, financially, personally, in their marriages, in their jobs, etc., need to be shown mercy. The world around us is much like the man who was beaten and robbed by the thieves in the story of the Good Samaritan in Luke 10:25-37. People need the Lord's mercy. Many have been beaten and broken by the effects of sin, theirs and others. They are sinking deep in their sins, however, many times we walk right by them on the 'other side' either by saying that they have made their bed so they must sleep in it, or we just ignore them and pretend that they don't exist.

Maybe you are a person who feels, toward the 'wounded', "Oh, just pull yourself up by the boot straps and move on!" Well, my friend, without Christ and without His divine help and guidance and without the love and power of His Spirit through His people, the world's 'boot straps' are paper thin to non-existent! They are helpless and need us to show God's love, grace and mercy towards them. The forgiven are to show mercy like we've been shown mercy. Let's never forget the ungrateful servant in Matthew 18:23-35.

Samaritans knew what it was like to be an outcast and to feel 'thrown-away'. Do we remember what it was like to be lost and without Jesus? As we recall where we were before Christ in our lives we should be drawn to be merciful as Christ was and is to us. Jesus, the "Good Samaritan" saw us on the road, but" "Beautiful, that's how mercy saw me. Though I was broken and so lost, mercy looked past all my faults; the justice of God saw all I had done, mercy saw me through the Son. Not as I was, but what I could be, that's how mercy saw me. May we today, this week and in the days to come have the same eyes.

CHAPTER ONE

THE MEANING OF MERCY AND THE MERCIFUL GOD

1.1. The Meaning of Mercy

So first of all let's look at what the mercy of God is. If you were to define mercy, it simply is infinite, inexhaustible energy of God. It is His infinite, inexhaustible energy to be compassionate! His mercy is the manifestation of His love. The arm of God's love is His mercy. It is the result and the effect of His goodness - the Lord is good: '...for he is good: for his mercy endures for ever'. His mercy is pity, He looks upon us and He pities us. His mercy is when He looks upon sin and He pities the guilt and the result of it, and He relieves!

Mercy is the unconditional love of God. Mercy is essentially God's relieving love poured out upon man in deep misery and trouble. Such affliction is spiritually rooted in the soul, though physical consequences are to be expected (Ps. 31:9-10; 32:3-4). Hence, when God's mercy relieves the soul, it may be expected that there will be attending physical benefits (Ps. 30:1-2; 107:19-20).

The Greek word used for "merciful" in this passage is the adjective *eleemon* (*el-eh-ay'-mone*). Although compassion, a feeling of sympathy, is part of mercy (*com* meaning "with", and passion meaning "suffering" so "with suffering"), mercy differs from compassion in that mercy is the active practice of compassion in the readiness to assist those in need. Therefore, the "merciful" are those who are not passive in showing love and compassion but who take an active role in bringing aid to those who suffer.

1.1.1. Mercy as an attribute of God, is not to be confounded with mere goodness.

This mistake is often made. That it is a mistake, you will see at once if you consider that mercy is directly opposed to justice, while yet justice is one of the natural and legitimate developments of goodness. Goodness may demand the exercise of justice; indeed it often does; but to say that mercy demands the exercise of justice, is to use the word without meaning. Mercy asks that justice be set aside. Of course mercy and goodness stand in very different relations to justice, and are very different attributes.

1.1.2. **Mercy is a disposition to pardon the guilty.**

Its exercise consists in arresting and setting aside the penalty of law, when that penalty has been incurred by transgression. It is, as has been said, directly opposed to justice. Justice treats every individual according to his deserts; mercy treats the criminal very differently from what he deserves to be treated. Desert is never the rule by which mercy is guided; while it is precisely the rule of justice.

1.1.3. **Mercy is exercised only where there is guilt. It always pre-supposes guilt.**

 The penalty of the law must have been previously incurred, else there can be no scope for mercy.

1.1.4. **Mercy can be exercised no farther than one's deserves punishment.**

It may continue its exercise just as long as punishment is deserved, but no longer; just as far as it desert goes, but no farther. If great punishment is deserved, great mercy can be shown; if endless punishment is due, there is then scope for infinite mercy to be shown, but not otherwise.

1.2.   **God is Merciful**

"The Lord is full of compassion and mercy" (James 5:11).

God's mercy is a monumental theme in Scripture, the English word appearing some 341 times in the Bible. Mercy and compassion are rooted in the very character of God. His law commands it. Wisdom teaches it. The prophets enjoin it and the Psalms applaud it. Of course, the fullest expression of the mercy of God is found in the person and work of Jesus Christ, the compassion of God incarnate. God is the master of mercy. His very nature desires to relieve you of the self-imposed misery and distress you experience because of your sin.

You find God's mercy in the Old Testament, you find it in the New Testament - in fact, you find God's mercy four times more in the Old Testament than you do within the New Testament. We must banish the thought that the God of Israel in the Old Testament is an angry God of justice, a God of judgment; but the God in the New Testament, is full of mercy and grace and love. But our God is an unchangeable God! He is the same yesterday, and today, and forever! Although the

New Testament, of course, is the full revelation of our God - and we don't know Him in all His mercy until we come into the New Testament - nevertheless God has always been, and always will be, a God of mercy.

1 Kings 3:6, we read that God's mercy is great. Psalm 86, we read that He is plenteous in mercy. Psalm 103, from everlasting to everlasting is His mercy. Luke 1, He is tender in mercy. He is abundant, overflowing, 1 Peter says. Ephesians, that we read says: 'But God, who is rich in mercy'. And Psalm 103:11 says, for as high as the heaven is above the earth - that's God's mercy! Immeasurable, unlimited, eternal, stretching from age to age. It is the mercy of God that is the tugboat that draws the sinner's foundering vessel into the arms of God. It's what saves the sinner, the mercy of God. It is what draws him to a Saviour, that's what he says: 'The Lord is merciful and gracious...long-suffering...abundant in goodness'. In fact, when you go into the book of the Revelation - and indeed throughout the Bible - God is pictured and represented as being a great King, sitting on a throne with a rainbow about His throne. The rainbow, of course, is a representation of the mercy of our God.

Have you ever thought about that? That God, in the Bible, in His great revelation of who He is, is represented more in mercy than in anger. Definitely the mercy of God is deeper than the depths of His wrath and His indignation, for He loves to be merciful! He is more inclined to mercy than He is to wrath. It was Watson, the old puritan, said: 'For God, acts of severity are rather forced from Him, He does not afflict willingly'. It's like the bee busily going from one flower and its pollen to another - and what is it doing? It is [making] honey because it naturally does that, and it goes from a flower to a flower and eventually it goes home, and there in the honeycomb it makes its honey - it's natural to it. But then when a young child happens to annoy it, it stings! It doesn't sting naturally, but only when it is provoked - and that's like our God. God is naturally merciful, but when God is provoked He will be angered, but He loves mercy rather than anger!

Mercy is said to be the work of God's right-hand - most of us are right-handed, and that's simply what the word of God means: that it is the thing that God likes to use the most, His mercy. He is more used to His right hand, He is more used to exercising mercy. God does not, in a sense, want to inflict punishment - indeed, in Isaiah 28, it is described as 'His strange work', it is strange for God to punish people, He is slow to anger. When He punishes a nation in the book of Isaiah it is said of Him that He: 'hired a razor to shave them' - imagine God hiring anything! You would think God wouldn't need to hire anything or borrow anything! But in Isaiah it says He hires a razor to shave them in anger and indignation - as if it's not His own, He has to borrow this part to do an act of wrath!

Just think for a moment: imagine how God would be if He had no mercy. Imagine what the holiness of God would be if there was no mercy. Imagine what the justice of God would be if mercy had no part in it. But the mercy of God overarches all His other attributes - and indeed, let me say this, that the mercy of God sweetens His other attributes. It's like old Moses, you remember, they came - the children of Israel - to the waters of bitterness and they couldn't drink from it, and what did Moses do? He cast the tree into the waters and made them sweet - and that is what the mercy of God is like to all His other attributes, it makes them sweet. It is one of His glories, it is one of the jewels in His crown - As we think about what it is to think right thoughts about God and contemplate God, we look at Exodus chapter 33 and we look at that wonderful encounter of communion of Moses with his God. He talked with God as a man talks with his friend, and we saw that in his brokenness, in his thirst after God - one who knew God in a way, perhaps, face-to-face that we will not know Him until we get to glory - he was able even to pray: 'Lord, show me your glory'! And the answer that was given back to Moses was this: 'I will make all my goodness pass before you, and I will show you mercy'.

That's what God wants to show to the world. In fact, even God's enemies receive mercy, it's like the dew that falls on the thistle as well as the rose. God's mercy - the sun shines on the righteous and on the unrighteous, and not just those that dwell in the presence of God. You remember Pharaoh, we read about him in this Psalm, as he was crossing the Red Sea pursuing, as a predator, after the Israelites - Pharaoh's head was crowned, and God had shown him mercy to put that crown upon his head. Even though his heart was hardened, his head was crowned! For the Lord, the word of God says, is good to all; the Lord is merciful to all.

That mercy is not shown to everyone! No, it's not. It's not shown to men who are rebellious, it's not shown to young people who are proud and say: 'I don't need the mercy of God' All humanity benefits from God's mercy to some degree. Jesus stated, "He gives His sunlight to both the evil and the good, and He sends rain on the just and on the unjust" (Matthew 5:45). But God also has a sovereign mercy He shows to those who are His. In gratitude, this is the mercy you are to share with others.

God shows you mercy because He compassionately cares about you. The prophet Isaiah states, "The Lord comforts His people and will have compassion on His afflicted ones" (Isaiah 49:13,). Your loving Father cares about what you are going through. The gospels are filled with examples of how Jesus was moved with compassion and acted to help those who were sick, suffering, and in need. Consider the blind man, Bartimaeus, or the ten lepers. Jesus reached out His hands and healed them. Or the woman caught in adultery. He spoke compassionately to her and forgave her.

To experience God's mercy, you must repent of your sin and accept God's forgiveness. The Bible promises, "The Lord our God is merciful and forgiving, even though we have rebelled against Him" (Daniel 9:9). God wants you in turn to be merciful to others. In the Sermon on the Mount, Jesus declared, "God blesses those who are merciful, for they will be shown mercy" (Matthew 5:7). In fact, Jesus said, "If you refuse to forgive others, your Father will not forgive your sins" (Matthew 6:15). God's mercy flows to those who show mercy to others.

Your loving heavenly Father is committed to your well-being. Out of His great compassion, He generously bestows on you His grace and mercy. God demonstrates His grace by showering you with blessings you do not deserve. He displays His great mercy by withholding the punishment you so rightfully deserve. "Let us come boldly to the throne of our gracious God. There we will receive His mercy, and we will find grace to help us when we need it" (Hebrews 4:16).

1.3. Biblical Passages Declaring God's Mercy

The LORD God, merciful and gracious, longsuffering, and abundant in goodness and truth (Exodus 34:6).

For the Lord thy God is a merciful God (Deuteronomy 4:31).

Let us fall now into the hand of the LORD; for his mercies are great (2 Samuel 24:14)

O give thanks unto the Lord; for he is good; for his mercy endures forever (1 Chronicles 16:34; Psalm 106:1, 107:1, 118:1, 136:1).

Good and upright is the Lord (Psalm 25:8).

For thou, Lord, art good, and ready to forgive; and plenteous in mercy unto all them that call upon thee (Psalm 86:5)

For the Lord is good, his mercy is everlasting (Psalm 100:5).

The Lord is merciful and gracious, slow to anger, and plenteous in mercy (Psalm 103:8)

The Lord is good to all, and his tender mercies are over all his works (Psalm 145:9).

I will not cause mine anger to fall upon you: for I am merciful, says the LORD, and I will not keep anger for ever (Jeremiah 3:12).

The LORD is good; for his mercy endures for ever (Jeremiah 33:11).

For he doth not afflict willingly nor grieve the children of men (Lamentations 3:33).

For he is gracious and merciful, slow to anger, and of great kindness (Joel 2:13).

Who is a God like unto thee, that pardons iniquity, and passes by the transgression of the remnant of his heritage? he retains not his anger for ever, because he delights in mercy (Micah 7:18)

Give all of you glory to him, because he is good, because his mercy endures for ever (Judith 13:21).
Blessed be God ... the Father of mercies (2 Corinthians 1:3).

For the Lord is very pitiful and of tender mercy (James 5:11).
God is love (1 John 4:16).

CHAPTER TWO
PROPERTIES OF GOD'S MERCY

The properties of God's mercy refer to the things to be considered respecting this attribute. The properties of God's mercy will lead more clearly into its nature, and the knowledge of it.

2.1. Mercy is an Attribute of God

Mercy is an attribute of God hence he is often described as "merciful", (Ex. 34:6; Neh. 9:17; Ps. 116:5). The Latin word "*Misericordia*" signifies, as one observes, having another's misery at heart; with whom it is no other than a propensity of his will to help persons in distress, whether in a temporal or spiritual way. This is one of the perfections which are in some measure imitable by creatures; "Be ye merciful as your Father is merciful" (Luke 6:36). But though God is merciful, it is not naturally and necessarily bore towards, and exercised on every object in misery: for then all would share in it, that are in misery, even all wicked men and devils; whereas it is certain they do not; but it is guided in the exercise of it by the love of God; and is governed and influenced by his sovereign will; who "has mercy on whom he will have mercy", (Rom. 9:15, 18) just as omnipotence is essential to God, but is not necessarily put forth to do everything it could; but is directed and guided by the will of God; who does whatsoever he pleases.

2.2. God's Mercy is Infinite

The mercy of God is infinite; as his nature is infinite, so are each of his attributes. His "understanding is infinite", (Ps. 147:5) and so his knowledge, wisdom, justice, holiness, and goodness, and likewise his mercy; it is so in its nature, and in its effects; and this appears both by bestowing an infinite good on men, which is Christ, who is the gift of God, and owing to the love, grace, and mercy of God; and who though, as man, is finite; yet, in his divine person, infinite; and as such given, (Isa. 9:6) and by his delivering them from an infinite evil, sin: sin, as an act of the creature, is finite; but objectively, infinite, as it is committed against God, the infinite Being, (Ps. 51:4) and therefore is not only infinite with respect to number, (Job 22:5) but with respect to its object, and also with respect to punishment for it; the demerit of it is eternal death; and this cannot be endured at once, or answered for in a short time; it is carried on "ad infinitum", without end; and therefore spoken of as everlasting and eternal. Now mercy has provided for the forgiveness of sin, and for the deliverance of men from the punishment of it, and from being liable to it (Heb. 8:12).

2.3. God's Mercy is Eternal

The mercy of God is eternal; the eternity of mercy is expressed in the same language as the eternity of God himself; see (Ps. 90:2, 103:17) it is from everlasting, as his love is; which is to be proved by the instances of it, called his "tender mercies", which "have been ever of old", or from everlasting, (Ps. 25:6) the council and covenant of peace were in eternity; in which the scheme of reconciliation to God was formed, and the method of it settled, which supposed them enemies, and so considered them as fallen creatures, and objects of mercy: and, indeed, the covenant of grace, which was from everlasting, is a superstructure of mercy, (Ps. 89:1-3) and since mercy is from everlasting, not anything in time can be the cause of it; not the misery of the creature, by the fall of Adam, nor works of righteousness done after conversion; nor the obedience and sufferings of Christ; things in time: and the mercy of God is to everlasting, in its fruits and effects; it is kept with Christ, and for him, the Mediator of the covenant; into whose hands are put all the promises and blessings of mercy; called, therefore, "the sure mercies of David", (Ps. 89:24, 28; Isa. 55:3) even temporal blessings, which flow from the mercy of God, are new every morning, and are daily continued; and spiritual ones always remain; the mercy of God never departs from his people, notwithstanding their backslidings; and though he chides them for them, and hides his face from them, yet still he has mercy on them (Ps. 89: 30-33; Isa. 54:6-10; Jer. 3:12,14).

2.4. God's Mercy is Immutable

The mercy of God is immutable, as he himself is, and his love also; and therefore the objects of it are not consumed, (Mal. 3:6) it is invariably the same in every state and condition into which they come; it is, as the Virgin Mary expresses it, "from generation to generation", without any variation or change (Luke 1:50).

2.5. Mercy is Ascribed to the Trinity

It is common to all the three divine persons, Father, Son, and Spirit; for as there is one common undivided essence, of which each equally partakes, the same divine perfections and attributes belong to them, and so this of mercy: mercy is ascribed to the God and Father of Christ, (1 Peter 1:3) and to our Lord Jesus Christ; not only as Man and Mediator, but as the true God and eternal life; to whose mercy we are to look for it, (Jude 1:21) and to the blessed Spirit, who helps the infirmities of the saints, "and makes intercession for them with groanings which cannot be uttered" (Rom. 8:26).

2.6. Mercy is Displayed in and Through Christ

Mercy is displayed in and through Christ; God out of Christ is a consuming fire; it is in him God proclaims his name, "a God gracious and merciful"; he is the mercy seat, and throne of grace, at which men obtain mercy and find grace; he is the channel through which it flows, and through whom it, in its effects, is conveyed to the sons of men: they are right who cast themselves not on the absolute mercy of God out of Christ; but upon his mercy, as displayed in him, as the Publican did (Luke 18:13). In a word, it is represented, as great, large, and ample, and very abundant; we read of a "multitude" of tender mercies; and God is said to be "rich" and "plenteous" in it; as will appear more fully by considering the objects and instances of it (Ps. 103:11, 51:1; 1 Peter 1:3; Eph. 2:4; Ps. 86:5).

2.7. Mercy is Guaranteed to Us

I have one last point to make about our merciful God and the free and abundant mercy he showers upon us. It is guaranteed. How refreshing therefore to hear that God's mercy is guaranteed. There is no question of doubt about that. Paul says to the Romans in 10.11 that As the Scripture says, "Anyone who trusts in him will never be put to shame." For there is no difference between Jew and Gentile—the same Lord is Lord of all and richly blesses all who call on him, for, "Everyone who calls on the name of the Lord will be saved." He is echoing Jesus' words "whoever comes to me I will never drive away".

Assurance, or rather lack of it, is one of the great problems for Christians today. Can you identify with that, the feeling of "I'm not sure...", or "Can God really love me....?", "Will it really work out in the end....?" God's mercy is guaranteed. We need to believe in the Bible. That is the problem we have when we lack assurance. It must be – the Bible tells us that God's mercy is assured. We feel sometimes it is not. What does that mean? We are doubting the Bible – we are unable to take God at his word. So let us see that God's mercy is guaranteed.

2.8. Mercy Comes to Us Without Limit

It is hard for us to imagine something without bounds. We have finite minds and we live in a finite world and the concept of infinity is pretty abstract. But God's mercy knows no bounds. Just think for a moment about the word "abundant". This language of abundance is found all through the Bible. Think about Ephesians again

– there Paul speaks about God's grace being "lavished upon us". Have you ever had anything lavished upon you? Or in Colossians he talks about the "glorious riches of the mystery which is Christ". "How wide and long and high and deep is the love of Christ" he writes to the Ephesians. In fact, so great is God's mercy that it is almost inexpressible. God's mercy knows no limit. There is none who is beyond his saving power. Why is this so important for us to grasp? Why, as we think about God's character, do we need to remind ourselves of the extent of God's mercy? The answer is, because of our need of it.

The Bible paints a very bleak picture of our lives without Christ. Let's not be under any illusion. We are dead, says Jesus. We are enslaved to sin, says Jesus. We are children of the Devil, says Jesus. Surely not! Yes, children of the Devil. Continuing without Christ would find us, literally in the depths of the grave. To be plucked from all of this requires something pretty special. Something big. Something without bounds. God's mercy. But there is still more we need to know about God as a merciful God. It's not enough to know that he is a God of mercy and that his mercy is unbounded. We need to know who it is available to. Who then is this great mercy available to?

2.9. Mercy is Available to All

The answer is, it is available to all. More precisely, it is available to all who call to God. God's mercy is free and available to all. The offer of grace is there for all who call on the name of the Lord. Brothers and sisters, Let us not limit God's mercy. We can do this In our minds, In our lives and in our church life. We feel deep down that there are certain people who are somehow beyond God's mercy. It is simply not true. It is available to all. If we are honest there are certain groups of people that if they walked in the back would make us feel uncomfortable. People with certain backgrounds. People with certain lifestyles. Sinners of all shapes, types, ages, sizes, orientations even! But God's mercy is available to all.

In 1 Timothy 2 we read how God wants all men to be saved. So his mercy is not limited. And he has given the Church the job of proclaiming that mercy, so our reaching out must not be limited. What is more, sometimes we limit the mercy of God in our own lives. No one, not one, is beyond God's mercy. It is not, however, a distribution without qualification. It does not come to everybody automatically. It is not a case of don't worry about anything, God's mercy will come to you. You need to do something – you need to call on the name of the Lord. We need to call on God's name. We need to tell others to do the same. We need to proclaim that is not enough to know God is a God of mercy. It is not enough to know the extent of that mercy – no, you must call on his name.

2.10. The Characteristic of God's mercy as described in the Bible

Great – Num. 14:18; Isa 54:7
Isaiah 54:7 "For a short time I abandoned you, but with great compassion I will gather you.
Rich – *Ephesians 2:4-5 4 But God, being rich in mercy, because of his great love with which he loved us, 5 even though we were dead in transgressions, made us alive together with Christ – by grace you are saved! –*
Manifold – Ne 9:27; Lam 3:32
Nehemiah 9:27 Therefore you delivered them into the hand of their adversaries, who oppressed them. But in the time of their distress they called to you, and you heard from heaven. In your abundant compassion you provided them with deliverers to rescue them from their adversaries.
Plenteous – Ps 86:5, 15; 103:8
Psalm 86:5 Certainly O Lord, you are kind and forgiving, and show great faithfulness to all who cry out to you.
Abundant – *1 Peter 1:3 Blessed be the God and Father of our Lord Jesus Christ! By his great mercy he gave us new birth into a living hope through the resurrection of Jesus Christ from the dead,*
Sure – Isa 55:3; Mic 7:20
Isaiah 55:3 Pay attention and come to me! Listen, so you can live! Then I will make an unconditional covenantal promise to you, just like the reliable covenantal promises I made to David.
Everlasting – I Chron 16:34; Ps 89:28; 106:1; 107:1; 136:1-26
1 Chronicles 16:34 Give thanks to the Lord, for he is good and his loyal love endures.
Tender – Ps 25:6; 103:4; Lu 1:78
Psalm 25:6 Remember your compassionate and faithful deeds, O Lord, for you have always acted in this manner.
New every morning - Lamentations *3:22-23 The Lord's loyal kindness never ceases; his compassions never end. They are fresh every morning; your faithfulness is abundant!*
High as heaven – Ps 36:5; 103:11
Psalm 36:5 O Lord, your loyal love reaches to the sky; your faithfulness to the clouds.

Filling the earth – *Psalm 119:64 O Lord, your loyal love fills the earth. Teach me your statutes!*
Over all his works – *Psalm 145:9 The Lord is good to all, and has compassion on all he has made.*

In the sending of Christ – *Luke 1:78 Because of our God's tender mercy the dawn will break upon us from on high*

In salvation – *Titus 3:5 he saved us not by works of righteousness that we have done but on the basis of his mercy, through the washing of the new birth and the renewing of the Holy Spirit,*

In long-suffering – Lam 3:22; Dan 9:9

Lamentations 3:22 The Lord's loyal kindness never ceases; his compassions never end.

To his people – Deut. 32:43; I Kings 8:23

Deuteronomy 32:43 Cry out, O nations, with his people, for he will avenge his servants' blood; he will take vengeance against his enemies, and make atonement for his land and people.

To them that fear Him – Ps 103:17; Luke 1:50

Luke 1:50 from generation to generation he is merciful to those who fear him.

To returning backsliders – Jer 3:12; Ho 14:4; Joel 2:13

Jeremiah 3:12 "Go and shout this message to my people in the countries in the north. Tell them, 'Come back to me, wayward Israel,' says the Lord. 'I will not continue to look on you with displeasure. For I am merciful,' says the Lord. 'I will not be angry with you forever.

To repentant sinners – Ps 32:5; Pr 28:13; Isa 55:7; Luke 15:18-20

Psalm 32:5 Then I confessed my sin; I no longer covered up my wrongdoing. I said, "I will confess my rebellious acts to the Lord." And then you forgave my sins. (Selah)

To the afflicted – Isa 49:13: 54:7

Isaiah 49:13 Shout for joy, O sky! Rejoice, O earth! Let the mountains give a joyful shout! For the Lord consoles his people and shows compassion to the oppressed.

To the fatherless – *Hosea 14:3 Assyria cannot save us; we will not ride warhorses. We will never again say, 'Our gods' to what our own hands have made. For only you will show compassion to Orphan Israel!"*

To whom He will – Ho 2:23; Rom 9:15, 18

Romans 9:15,18 15 For he says to Moses: "I will have mercy on whom I have mercy, and I will have compassion on whom I have compassion."… 18 So then, God has mercy on whom he chooses to have mercy, and he hardens whom he chooses to harden.

God's mercy is a ground of Hope – Ps 130:7; 147:11

Psalm 130:7 O Israel, hope in the Lord, for the Lord exhibits loyal love, and is more than willing to deliver.

God's mercy is a ground of trust – *Psalm 52:8 But I am like a flourishing olive tree in the house of God; I continually trust in God's loyal love.*

God's mercy should be:

Sought for ourselves - *Psalm 6:2 Have mercy on me, Lord, for I am frail! Heal me, Lord, for my bones are shaking!*
Sought for others – Ga 6:16; I Tim 1:2; II Tim 1:18
1 Timothy 1:2 to Timothy, my genuine child in the faith. Grace, mercy, and peace from God the Father and Christ Jesus our Lord!
Pleaded in prayer – Ps 6:4; 25:6; 51:1
Psalm 51:1 For the music director; a psalm of David, written when Nathan the prophet confronted him after David's affair with Bathsheba. Have mercy on me, O God, because of your loyal love! Because of your great compassion, wipe away my rebellious acts!
Rejoiced in – *Psalm 31:7 I will be happy and rejoice in your faithfulness, because you notice my pain and you are aware of how distressed I am.*
Magnified – I Chron. 16:34; Ps 115:1; 118:1-4,29; Jer 33:11
Psalm 118:1-4 1 Give thanks to the Lord, for he is good and his loyal love endures! 2 LetIsrael say, "Yes, his loyal love endures!" 3Let the family of Aaron say, "Yes, his loyal love endures!" 4 Let the loyal followers of the Lord say, "Yes, his loyal love endures!"
God's mercy is exemplified in
Lot - *Genesis 19:16, 19 16 When Lot hesitated, the men grabbed his hand and the hands of his wife and two daughters because the Lord had compassion on them. They led them away and placed them outside the city...19 Your servant has found favor with you, and you have shown me great kindness by sparing my life.*
Epaphroditus - *Philippians 2:27 In fact he became so ill that he nearly died. But God showed mercy to him – and not to him only, but also to me – so that I would not have grief on top of grief.*
Paul - *1 Timothy 1:13 even though I was formerly a blasphemer and a persecutor, and an arrogant man. But I was treated with mercy because I acted ignorantly in unbelief,*

CHAPTER THREE
OBJECTS OF GOD'S MERCY

The objects of mercy may be next observed: and that this may appear in a plain and clear light, it will be proper to remark, that the **mercy of God is general and special**.

3.1. The General Mercy of God

With respect to the **general mercy of God,** all creatures are the objects of it; "the Lord is good to all, and his tender mercies are over all his works", (Ps. 145:9) there is not a creature in all the earth but partakes of it; hence says the Psalmist, "The earth, O Lord, is full of thy mercy!" (Ps. 119:64) even the brute creation, the mute animals, share in it; it is owing to mercy that they are preserved in their beings, (Ps. 36:5, 6) and that a provision of food is made for their sustenance; and who sometimes are in great distress, and when they cry to God he gives them their food, (Joel 1:18-20; Ps. 104:27, 28, 147:9; Job 38:41). All men, good and bad, partake of the providential goodness and mercy of God; he is kind to the unthankful and unholy, and makes the sun to rise on the evil and on the good, and sends rain on the just and on the unjust (Luke 6:35; Matthew 5:45). He preserves and supports all men in their beings, and so is the Saviour of all, and especially of them that believe, (1 Tim. 4:10) and gives them the necessaries of life, food and raiment, and all things richly to enjoy, both for convenience and pleasure: yea, even the devils themselves partake of mercy, in some sense; for though God has not spared them, so as to save them, and not condemn them; yet he has given them a kind of reprieve, and reserved them to the judgment of the great day; so that they are not yet in full torments, as their sins have deserved; and as God punishes none more but less than their sins require, this may be reasonably supposed to be the case of devils, even hereafter.

3.2. The Special Mercy of God

As to the **special mercy of God,** none are the objects of that but elect men, who are called "vessels of mercy", (Rom. 9:23) because they are filled with it, even with all spiritual blessings, which flow from it, and which are bestowed on them according as they are chosen in Christ, (Eph. 1:3, 4) and so particularly regeneration, which is according to the abundant mercy of God, they are favoured with, being the elect of God, (1 Peter 1:2, 3) and these, as they are redeemed by Christ, share in the special mercy and goodness of God; and therefore are under obligation to say, with wonder and thankfulness, "the Lord is good; his mercy endures for ever", (Ps. 107:1, 2) and especially, being effectually called by the grace of God, they appear to be the objects of mercy; then they who "had not obtained mercy", did not know their interest in it, nor actually enjoyed the blessings of it, "now have obtained mercy"; are blessed both with knowledge of interest in it, and with the open possession of the blessings of it (1 Peter 2:10). These are described sometimes by them "that call upon" the Lord, to whom he is plenteous in mercy, (Ps. 86:5) by "them that love him, and keep his commandments; to whom he shows his mercy", (Ex. 20:6; Neh. 1:5; Dan. 9:4) and by them that fear him, and towards whom his mercy always is (Ps. 103:11, 13, 17). Not that calling upon God, love to him, and observance of his commands, and the fear of him, are the causes of his mercy to them, since that is prior to all these, and is the cause of them; but these describe the persons who openly, and manifestly, share in the mercy of God, and to whom the effects of it have been applied, and who may expect a continuance of it, and larger discoveries and displays thereof to be made unto them; as well as they show that the mercy of God is special and distinguishing, and yet that it is not limited to any family or nation, but is enjoyed by all that love and fear the Lord in every nation (Acts 10:34, 35).

CHAPTER FOUR
INSTANCES OF GOD'S MERCY

The instances of mercy, to the objects of it, are many and various.

4.1. God's Mercy Appears in Election

It appears in election: it is, indeed, a controversy among theologians, whether election is an act of love or of mercy: I am inclined to be of the opinion of those who take it to be an act of love, and not mercy; as God chose literal Israel, because he loved them, (Deut. 7:7, 8) so spiritual Israel are first beloved, and then chosen, (2 Thess. 2:13) "*electio praesupponit dilectionem*"; but then, though the decree of election flows from love, and not mercy; yet God has in it decreed to show mercy; he has resolved within himself, saying, "I will have mercy, and will save"; and therefore in this decree he has appointed them not unto wrath, which they deserve, but to obtain salvation by Christ; which supposes them fallen creatures, and so objects of mercy; for the decree of election may be distinguished into the decree of the end and the decree of the means: with respect to the end, the glory of God, men were considered as unfallen, in the pure mass out of which God designed to make them for himself: but with respect to the means, redemption by Christ, and faith in him, the Redeemer, and sanctification of the Spirit; here they were considered as fallen creatures; and so, with propriety, those chosen ones may be called vessels of mercy.

4.2. God's Mercy is Displayed in the Covenant of Grace
The covenant of grace is a display of the mercy of God, as before observed; it is built upon mercy, and built up with it; it is stored with it, and is full of it. Mercy called Christ to engage in it, and set him up as the Mediator of it, and came before him with the blessings of goodness: the provisions of Christ, as a Redeemer and Saviour in it; of forgiveness of sins through his blood; and of reconciliation and atonement by his sacrifice; and of regeneration and sanctification by his Spirit, are so many displays of mercy.

4.3. God's Mercy is Displayed in the Redemption

You can witness the mercy of God in redemption. Imagine this: the mercy of God without the atonement of Christ. Can you imagine that? I can't. The mercy of God is impotent without Calvary. It has no power, it's no good to you. God has no mercy apart from Calvary! For it was the mercy seat. In the Old Testament, the Ark of the covenant - the lid that was on top of it - wasn't it called the mercy seat? And that was the God-appointed place where Moses would commune with God, that's the place where the high priest, once a year on the Day of the Atonement, would sprinkle the blood, that was the place associated with covering and the removal of sin - through the blood God has mercy! The Lord Jesus Christ is His mercy seat. You see, Calvary is where God meets the sinner and extends mercy. Wasn't it said, prophetically, of our Lord Jesus Christ in the Psalms, 85: 'Mercy and truth are met together; righteousness and peace have kissed each other' - the mercy seat! Have you been there? Have you been to Calvary?

Redemption itself is a signal instance of the mercy of God. Mercy resolved upon the redemption and salvation of the elect; being viewed as fallen in Adam, and as sinners, mercy provided a Redeemer and Saviour of them, and laid their help upon him; mercy called Christ to undertake the work of redemption, and engaged him in it; mercy sent him, in the fullness of time, to visit them, and perform it; mercy delivered them up into the hands of justice and death, in order to obtain it, and it is most illustriously glorified in it; "mercy and truth have met together", (Ps. 85:10) yea, Christ himself, in his love and pity, has redeemed his people (Isa. 63:9).

4.4. God's Mercy is Clearly Shown in the Forgiveness of Sins

The forgiveness of sin is another instance of the mercy of God, to which it is frequently ascribed (Ps. 51:1; Dan. 9:9; Luke 1:77, 78). God has promised it in covenant, as the effect of his mercy; "I will be merciful to their unrighteousness" (Heb. 8:12). He has set forth Christ, in his purposes, to be the propitiation for the remission of sins; and has sent him, in time, to shed his blood for it, (Rom. 3:25) and it is the mercy of God, which is the foundation of hope of it; and encourages sensible sinners to ask, and through which they obtain it (Ps. 103:8; Luke 18:13; 1 Tim. 1:13).

4.5. God's Mercy Brings us forgiveness

Ephesians 2.4 tells us that fundamentally God's mercy is about forgiveness. It is a fundamental and prime requirement. People all around the world are thinking the same thing. They are thinking that they will be able to approach God on their own merit. It's human nature to think that way. It's human nature to be proud but what the Bible does is shatter our illusions. And they are illusions. Even your very best, your absolute best, is not enough to please God – that is what Paul writes to the Romans, "those controlled by the sinful nature cannot please God" (Romans 8.8). And so, if we are to ever have a relationship with God our prime need, our first need is this – to be forgiven.

Whatever else our needs may be, and they may be many, don't get me wrong, our most important need is to be forgiven. David knew this. He is in deep trouble – yet is appealing to God's forgiving nature in Psalm 51. Yes, God will certainly help us in other areas of our lives – but first and foremost we need to see our need of forgiveness which comes from a merciful God. Sin is a relationship breaker. Goodness, how we know that in our own lives, don't we. How many times, if you can even count them, has sin caused you problems and difficulties in relationships. We know that is true. How much more so in our relationship with the Lord of all. Sin is a relationship breaker.

However, God's mercy means that he does not treat us as our sins deserve. That is the message of Psalm 103.10 –those exact words "he does not treat us as our sins deserve, or repay us according to our iniquities". Think about that for a moment. Where would you be if it wasn't for God's mercy. You would not have woken up this morning. You and I are deserving of judgment. We are deserving of destruction and punishment and condemnation. But God's mercy means that we are not treated as our sins deserve. God's mercy means we can be forgiven.

Imagine for a moment a court room. It's a well known scene isn't it. We often think about God's final judgment as being like a court room scene, and that is often the way it is described in the Bible. Now, imagine you are trying to argue your case for acceptance by God and entry into his new kingdom. What would you say? The invitation comes from the judge sitting there at the front, it's an invitation given to Israel in Isaiah, "review the past for me", says the judge, "let us argue the matter together, state the case for your innocence".

How ridiculous to imagine that we could stand in such a court and argue the case with God. Yet that is how many of us lived, how perhaps many of us continue to live – on our own merits. In that same passage in Isaiah 43, God gives the damning verdict, "your first father sinned; your spokesmen rebelled against me". The verdict is "guilty as charged". And yet, that same passage in Isaiah also speaks of God's mercy, "I, even I, am he who blots out your transgressions for my own sake and remembers your sin no more."

God's mercy means forgiveness for wicked, sinful people like you and me. How we need to know the God of mercy! However, it is not enough to know that God's mercy brings forgiveness. We need to have some idea of the extent of his mercy. You see, if God's mercy only forgives a little, we are in deep trouble. That is what we are like sometimes isn't it? We can forgive a little, but we find it hard to forgive much. If that is true of God's mercy, then I am in serious trouble.

4.6. God's Mercy is Displayed in Regeneration

The mercy of God is displayed in regeneration, to which that is ascribed in (1 Peter 1:3) and it is wonderful and special mercy, to quicken a sinner dead in trespasses and sins; to enlighten such that sit in darkness, and in the shadow of death; to deliver from the bondage of Satan those, that are led captive by him at his will; to snatch them as brands out of the burning, and save from everlasting fire; to bring men out of a pit, wherein there was no water, no relief and comfort, and in which they must otherwise die; and to reveal Christ to them, and in them, the hope of glory; and give them a good hope, through grace, of being forever happy. These are some of the great and good things which God does for his people in the effectual calling, having compassion on them.

You know it in regeneration, I hope to God it's happened to you! Like Paul on that road to Damascus, he had no thought of God - that's what he says! He was in ignorance of who the Christ was, and he's walking down that road going to kill Christians, going as the enemy of God - and out of the blue God arrests him! And God lets the scales fall from off his eyes, to see his sin - that is the special mercy of God, to be pitied, to be rescued from judgment and hell. And let me say this today: that mercy is not shown to everyone! No, it's not. It's not shown to men who are rebellious, it's not shown to young people who are proud and say: 'I don't need the mercy of God' - for the word of God says in Luke 1: 'His mercy is on them that fear Him'! If you don't fear God, you'll know nothing of the mercy of God. Listen sinners, Romans says: 'Not by works of righteousness, but according to His mercy He saved us. So then it is not of him that runs, but of God that shows mercy'! Do you know the mercy of God? If you don't know the mercy of God my friend, it's because of your proud, bold, sinful, deep dyed, damnable heart!

This special mercy, God lavishes it upon whom He wills who has faith in Him. This is a sovereign thing, this is the God of all gods who says in Romans 9: 'For he said to Moses, I will have mercy on whom I will have mercy, and I will have compassion on whom I will have compassion...Therefore he shows mercy on whom he will have mercy, and whom he will harden'. This is a baffling thing, that the Lord harden men against Him? Now don't be confused about this, because men are very responsible for every single thing that they do - and let me say that God doesn't make a man evil, God doesn't make a man reject Him, that is given to your own individual choice. But let me say this: when God Almighty, the sovereign God decides to withdraw His influence in grace from your heart, your heart will harden! Oh, that men would know this! That if God decided to take His gracious sunshine away from your heart, He wouldn't need to harden your heart...it would harden itself. It's like when the sun sets, the temperature goes down and the frost comes across the road. You wouldn't dream of saying that, because the sun has gone out, that the sun hardened the ground. Did the sun harden the ground? No! But that gracious influence of God, that is why we say to you today - in the light of the Gospel - Pharaoh hardened his own heart! Because God took His grace away from him, his heart became hard - and God says to you today: if you hear His voice, harden not your heart! How terrible that on that judgement day, if you should stand before the Lord Jesus Christ, and it would be the mercy of God that would indict you! Imagine that! The very goodness of God would damn your soul, because you rejected it!

If you hear His voice, harden not your heart! How terrible that on that judgement day, if you should stand before the Lord Jesus Christ, and it would be the mercy of God that would indict you! Imagine that! The very goodness of God would damn your soul, because you rejected it!

4.7. Complete Salvation and Eternal Life itself, flow from the God's Mercy
Complete salvation, and eternal life itself, flow from the mercy of God; he saves, "not by works of righteousness, but according to his mercy", (Titus 3:5) and when he shall put his people into the full possession of salvation, then they shall find and obtain mercy in that day, even in the day of judgment, when they shall go into life eternal; and therefore are now directed to look unto the mercy of Christ for it, (2 Tim. 1:18; Jude 1:21).

4.8. God's Mercy is in All Life
His mercy is in all life. Secondly, His mercy is in our circumstances. Now, you believers this is for you. Psalm 103 says: 'For as the heaven is high above the earth, so great is [God's] mercy toward them that fear him'. 'To us', Corinthians says, 'He is the Father of mercies' - that means this, believer: everything in your life, every circumstance, everything that has happened to you, there is the mercy of God in it! It is of the Lord's mercies that we are not consumed, is it not? God's mercy is never absent, God's mercy is never invisible, it's never empty - and what a humbling thing, that even in our trials and our tribulations the God of mercy has His hand in it.

4.9. God's Mercy is Witnessed in Hell

God's mercy is seen in all, it's seen in your circumstances, it's seen redemption - and let me say this very soberingly, and this has shook me as I've been studying this: God's mercy is witnessed in hell. That's a strange thing, isn't it? Even, think of it, when the lost are cast into the lake of fire it is an act of God's mercy. It's not from your point of view, if you're not saved - but from heaven's point of view it is.

You see, hell is the casting out forever of all sin. Forever! And is it not the mercy of God that in the new Jerusalem we read that there shall in no wise enter into it anything that defiles, neither whatsoever works abomination? Can you imagine walking down the streets of gold and hearing blasphemy in one ear, and hearing the name of the Lord thy God taken in vain in the other? Can you imagine that? No! The mercy of God is towards the righteous - those who believe - so much that God won't have it, and every sin is damned in hell.

It's awesome to think, as we read in 136, that God overthrew Pharaoh and his hosts in the Red Sea for His mercy endures forever. How could anybody say the like of that? That's their song of praise! 'God overthrew Pharaoh in the Red Sea, for His mercy endures forever', for it was the mercy of God. We read in Revelation 19- John says: 'I heard a great voice of much people in heaven, saying, Alleluia; Salvation, and glory, and honour, and power, unto the Lord our God: For true and righteous are his judgments: for he has judged the great whore, which did corrupt the earth with her fornication, and has avenged the blood of his servants at her hand. And again they said, Alleluia. And her smoke rose up for ever and ever'! That's like saying: 'Praise the Lord, the damned are damned'. Even the mercy of God in the likes of that? Do you know what that tells me? If I was a sinner, without Christ it would tell me of the foolishness of those who believe that God's mercy will see them through the end. 'I'll take a chance. I've lived alright, I haven't done anybody any harm. I go to my church, I try my best, I'm good to my family - God would never cast me into hell! His mercy endures forever!' - that is to forget, my friend, that He's a God of justice, that He's sovereign in His mercy - and if you hear His voice, for God's sake harden not your heart, for God may withdraw His grace and His mercy and you'll be lost! God says: 'I will by no means clear the guilty'. He says: 'The wicked shall be turned into hell, and all the nations that forget God'.

Imagine a man or a woman, and they don't wash themselves, they don't clean their teeth and their teeth are rotten, they don't wash themselves and there are germs crawling over them - all over their hair and everything, under their nails - and they are getting diseased because of it. Do you think God would withhold disease from a man or a woman that lived in that condition? Not on your life! Do you think God will lavish His mercy on a soul that has heaped sin upon its own head? I don't know what kind of a God that is, but it's not our God! Do you know something? You can make God's mercy your enemy. Like sucking poison out of a beautiful flower, you can have a deadly, deadly blow dealt to your soul!

CHAPTER FIVE

APPLICATION OF GOD'S MERCY

5.1. We Must See Our Need of Mercy

 we must see our need of God's mercy. When you list the great people of the Bible, don't you include David? I do. A great man. A man who God said "was after his own heart". What a great accolade! But just think – if David needed God's mercy, don't you? Not just saving mercy either, but God's mercy every day, unless of course you have found a way to live a perfect life!

5.2. We Need to Trust God's Mercy

You ought to trust God's mercy. Isn't that right? That's what the Psalmist said: 'I will trust in the mercy of God for ever'. Listen! Will you please think about this: the mercy of God, right now, here and now, is a fountain open - and if you would just let your bucket of faith drop down, you could take a draught, and drink by faith of that well of salvation. If you're not saved, well, listen to me: God's mercy is open for you now - it'll not be open forever, but it's open now! It's open now and the Lord Jesus says, 'whosoever will, let him come and take of the water of life freely'. Imagine going to court and there's a judge there, and the judge is pleading with the person in the dock! Have you ever seen that? I've never seen it! The judge pleading with the person accused? But this is your Judge pleading with you to partake of His mercy. My friend, this is baffling! Imagine the fool that would refuse such a thing! God is saying to you, in His mercy: 'Allow Me to love you, be willing to let Me save you!' - mercy pleases God! But unbelief smothers it, and if you're not a believer, the bowels of God's compassion are shut up for you, the wounds gaping and the sore of the Saviour that flow forth that medicine for all sin and shame and iniquity are closed over for you. There is no compassion, there is no joy, there is no virtue in the wounded Christ for you! Will you trust Him? Now come on! Will you? Such great mercy enduring forever! Will you partake of it?

5.3. We Need To Obtain Mercy

We ought to obtain mercy. Yes, you can show it, yes, you can trust in it - but you know, we can obtain it. We can go in prayer to God and look at Him - not in robes of justice and robes of wrath, but we can see God clad and arched in a rainbow of mercy. Imagine coming to a God such as that, a God whose mercy is toward us - that should add wings to our prayers, to know that God is so great, God is so mighty yet God is for us. We ought to come boldly before our God, knowing that He is merciful. My Christian friend it should be blatantly obvious to you that if you come to God you will obtain mercy.

It says of Samuel that on one occasion he took a suckling lamb before God - and every believer in this place, if you could take the Lamb of God in your arms, slain before God, into His presence knowing that it's through that Lamb that you come; if you would come to the throne of grace on His perfect merits and His finished work you would hear this: 'My child, you have not a high priest which cannot be touched with the feelings of your infirmities, but He was in all points tested like as you are - yet without sin. Therefore, My child, come boldly unto the throne grace that [you] may obtain mercy!' - to obtain mercy and find grace to help in time of need.

If you come to Christ now, in the day of salvation, you will know the mercy of God - but if you reject it will be the very thing that will damn your soul. Will you come? Child of God, things are hard, things have been difficult - but whatever you do, throughout it all don't miss the mercy of God in it, for if we didn't have it we would be consumed - but great is His faithfulness. Rest upon it today, and if you're broken hearted, reach out by faith to that throne boldly, and obtain mercy that you need.

5.4. We Must Appeal God's Mercy

we must appeal to God's mercy. We need to learn to pray with arguments. We need to learn to express the reasons why God should answer our prayers affirmatively, he said. It's no good just knowing about God's mercy – let's make it the central point of our prayer! We need to be like David. Our sin is great. But God's mercy is greater. Our sin is enormous, yet God's mercy is boundless. Our sin drives a wedge between ourselves and God, yet God's mercy is freely available to all who call on him and comes with a solid, lifetime guarantee. So call on him. Whether you have never done so before or not. However long you have followed him, appeal and call on his mercy today.

5.5. We Must Proclaim Mercy

we must proclaim God's mercy. If we are in need of God's mercy so is the world. So is our land. So is our town. So are our road, our neighbours, friends and relatives. How will they hear unless we tell them?

5.6. We Need to Exemplify Mercy in our Lives

But the God of mercy and compassion also calls His people to exemplify these attributes in their own lives. As God has been merciful to us, we bear forth the image of this mercy to the world. We are called to "give justice to the weak and the fatherless; to maintain the right of the afflicted and the destitute. Rescue the weak and the needy; and to deliver them from the hand of the wicked" (Ps. 82:3–4).

You ought to show mercy. That's what the Lord said in the beatitudes, isn't it? Matthew 5:7: 'Blessed are the merciful: for they shall obtain mercy'. James 2:13: 'For he shall have judgment without mercy, that hath showed no mercy' - if you don't show any mercy in your life, God will judge you without any mercy. Luke 6:36: 'Be ye therefore merciful, as your Father also is merciful' - show mercy one to another!

CHAPTER SIX
CONDITIONS FOR RECEIVING GOD'S MERCY

The mistakes into which many fall concerning the obtenance of God's mercy are many. Many trust professedly in the mercy of God without fulfilling the conditions on which only, mercy can be shown. They may hold on in such trusting till they die-but no longer. Many are defending their own salvation by self justification and Pleas that excuse self. A sinner cannot find mercy in this state.

Some are covering up their sins, yet dream of going to heaven. Do they think they can hide those sins from the Omniscient Eye? Do they think to cover their sins and yet it "prospers," despite of God's awful word? We cannot reasonably ask for mercy beyond our acknowledged and felt guilt, and they mistake fatally who suppose that they can. Without a deep conviction of conscious guilt we cannot be honest and in earnest in supplicating mercy.

6.1. A Conviction of Guilt

None can properly be said to trust in the mercy of God unless they have committed crimes, and are conscious of this fact. Justice protects the innocent, and they may safely appeal to it for defence or redress. But for the guilty nothing remains but to trust in mercy. Trusting mercy always implies a deep heartfelt conviction of personal guilt.

6.2. We Must Repent

Certainly no sinner has the least ground to hope for mercy until he repents. Will God pardon the sinner while yet in his rebellion? Never. To do so would be most unjust in God-most ruinous to the universe. It would be virtually proclaiming that sin is less than a trifle-that God cares not how set in wickedness the sinner's heart is; he is ready to take the most rebellious heart, unhumbled, to his own bosom. Before God can do this he must cease to be holy.

6.3. We Must Confess our Sins

He that confesses and he only, "shall find mercy." God sustains such relations to the moral universe that he cannot forgive without the sinner's confession. He must have the sinner's testimony against himself and in favour of law and obedience.

Let it be understood that before we can trust in the mercy of God, we must really repent and make our confession as public as we have made our crime.

6.4. We Must Really Make Restitution

We must really make restitution so far as lies in our power. Restitution is giving back what you took. It is repairing the damage caused. It is returning stolen money or goods to the individual. Restitution is the art of returning or restoring to a person something or right of which he has been unjustly deprived. Genuine repentance leads to a desire to redress wrongs, making restorations wherever possible. The idea of "whenever possible" is crucially important to remember. There are some crimes and sins for which there is no adequate restitution. In such instances, the Christian should make some form of restitution that demonstrates repentance.

6.5. We Must Really Reform

Reformation is the act of correction or amendment of life, manners, or anything vicious or corrupt. It is the change from worse to better, one's behavior or lifestyles. Amendment of life is very necessary to obtain God's mercy, One cannot continue in bad behavior or sin or a life of disobedience to the commandments of God and still expect to be forgiven by God. Amendment of life involves abandoning former bad behaviors, sins and lifestyles that offend God and man. It involves strong decisions, avoiding occasions of sin, avoiding at times some places, some people, some things, some addictions in order to please God.

6.6 Align with the Plan of Salvation

This plan is based on the assumption that we deserve everlasting death and must be saved, if ever, by sovereign grace and mercy. Nothing can save but mercy-mercy which meets the sinner in dust, prostrate, without an excuse or an apology, giving to God all the glory and taking to himself all the guilt and shame. There is hope for you, sinner, in embracing this plan with all the heart.

It is not the greatness of our sins, but our pride of heart that forbids our salvation. It is not anything in our past life, but it is our present state of mind that makes our salvation impossible. Think of this. You see very clearly why all are not saved. It is not because God is not willing to save all, but because they defeat the effort God makes to save them. They betake themselves to every possible refuge and subterfuge; resist conviction of guilt, and repel every call of mercy.

Dying sinner, you may just as well have mercy today as not. All your past sins present no obstacle at all if you only repent and take the offered pardon. Your God proffers your life. "As I live, says the Lord, I have no pleasure in your death." Why will you reject such offered life? And will you still persist? Indeed, if there ever was anything that filled the universe with astonishment, it is the sinner's rejection of mercy.

CHAPTER SEVEN

CHRISTIAN MERCY

"The wisdom that descends from above is full of mercy and good fruits."
Matthew 5:7. *Blessed are the merciful, for they shall obtain mercy.*

The beatitudes with which our Lord commences his incomparable Sermon on the Mount, were intended to correct the errors which the Jews entertained as to the nature of his kingdom; and to exhibit to the world the leading features of the religion which he came to promulgate. Mistaking the spirit of prophecy, and interpreting literally the imagery by which, in the glowing style of Oriental composition, the writers of the Old Testament had described the person, reign, and success of Messiah—the Jews expected a mighty general, who at the head of victorious armies, would break the Roman yoke from their necks, and raise their nation into the proud pre-eminence of universal dominion. If such expectations had been well-founded, it is evident that lofty ambition, militaristic courage, indignant contempt of others, unrelenting severity, and insatiable resentment would have been the prominent virtues of the disciple of Christ. The dispositions which I have just enumerated, formed, in fact, the popular characters of the age in which our Lord appeared, both among Jews and Gentiles. And indeed the 'hero' has been a far greater favorite than the 'saint' with the historian of every age and every country. The mild and passive virtues have few admirers—compared with those which appear invested with the dazzling splendor of state policy, restless ambition, and military prowess.

But 'the kingdom of Christ is not of this world'—a remark which will strictly apply to his subjects; and to delineate their character as well as to describe their blessedness—was the design of the beautiful discourse with which he opened his public ministry. Instead of that proud consciousness of superiority which both the Jews and Gentiles entertained—the disciples of Christ would be characterized by a deep sense of their needs and imperfections, and the most unfeigned humility, "Blessed are the poor in spirit." Instead of being mirthful, thoughtless and fickle, addicted to scenes of festivity and noisy mirth—they would be serious, thoughtful, and penitent, "Blessed are those who mourn." Instead of entertaining that high sense of personal importance, which is quick to receive offence, and hasty to resent it—they would meekly bear injuries, and rather forgive than revenge them, "Blessed are the meek."

Instead of an insatiable thirst after conquest—they would ardently covet the victory over their own lusts and corruptions, "Blessed are those who hunger and thirst after righteousness." Instead of delighting in the horrors of war, in order to gather the ensanguined laurel from the field of battle—they would be infinitely better pleased to sympathize with the sorrows of mankind, and relieve them, "Blessed are the merciful." Instead of seeking their happiness in luxurious or sensual gratifications—they would find it in the growth of inward purity, "Blessed are the pure in heart."

Instead of fomenting and delighting in hostility, either domestic, social or national—they would sacrifice everything but principle, to restore harmony where it has been unfortunately lost, and to maintain it where it is possessed, "Blessed are the peacemakers." Instead of coveting the gale of popular applause by sacrificing their convictions to the smiles of the world—they would endure its bitterest wrath rather than apostatize from the faith; and esteem themselves more happy in securing the crown of martyrdom than a high place in the verses of the poet, or the declamations of the orator, "Blessed are those who are persecuted for righteousness sake."

Such is Christianity—as its Author has described and blessed it. Such is the model after which every Christian character ought to be formed. How far short of this we fall, I blush to think. It is high time we should return to first principles, and begin, as for the first time, to enquire in what true practical religion really consists. From this assemblage of holy graces I select for our present consideration the most useful of them all. My subject is, **Christian Mercy**—in the discussion of which, I shall explain its nature, direct to its objects, enumerate its properties, unfold its reward, and urge its practice.

7.1. The NATURE of Christian Mercy.

Mercy may be defined to be that benevolent sorrow which we feel at perceiving the sufferings or approaching calamities of others, connected with a desire to relieve them. The object of mercy is simple 'misery'—not according to some ethical writers as the effect of guilt—but as misery, without considering the cause which has produced it.

7.1.1. Mercy is that benevolent sorrow which we feel at perceiving the sufferings or approaching calamities of others.

Without such a compassionate disposition, a man cannot be merciful. He may be liberal in the distribution of his wealth, but this may arise from ostentation, or may be an operation of self-righteousness. To the possession of the amiable and useful virtue of which I am now treating, a tender sympathizing heart is indispensably necessary. There must be a cord in the bosom vibrating to every note of woe, and where this exists in connection with a desire to relieve, there is mercy—even though the means of relief are not possessed. One may be destitute of mercy, while lavishing thousands; another may possess mercy in high perfection, and yet not have money to bestow. Mercy begins in sympathy, although it does not end there. It is in the heart that mercy erects her throne; it is thence she issues her commands, and dispenses her favors—the senses and the bodily members are her servants; the gold and the silver are her means. But mercy never leaves the heart—for when she has left that she has departed from the character.

7.1.2. Mercy is always connected with a desire to relieve misery, and that this desire will always prompt to vigorous exertion.

Right dispositions wherever they prevail in the heart, will always appear by their appropriate effects in the conduct. Dr. Hartley concisely defines compassion "to be that uneasiness which a man feels at sight of the misery of another," and mercy, if not synonymous with compassion, is so near akin to it, as to admit of a very similar definition. If the misery of another renders us uneasy, a regard to our own peace will make us either anxious to relieve it, or to avoid the sight of it; the latter is the case with the man who merely feels the sorrows of others, but has no genuine compassion; the former is the conduct of the merciful. Mercy is a passion—but it leads to action. It is not mere sentimentalism, which sighs and weeps—yet does nothing more; like that of Sterne, which led him to shed tears on the sufferings of an expiring animal, but permitted him to leave his own mother in a state bordering on starvation. 'I feel for you' is a common reply to the tale of the sufferer; but unless that feeling be so far excited as to grant relief—it is not true compassion. James by an admirable association of ideas, has told us that the wisdom which comes from above is full of mercy and good fruits—evidently teaching us that this tender and beautiful grace of mercy, is never seen in its right character, but when in a state of fructification. And what are its fruits? Kind words? Sorrowful looks? Tears of pity? No! These are its blossoms, but substantial acts of kindness are the fruits which the 'hand of misery' is invited to pluck from this heavenly plant for its own relief.

We must renounce our claims to be a merciful person, unless there is a **desire**, and that desire be followed by vigorous **exertion**, to relieve the misery which has excited our sympathy. A person of mild and gracious manners, soft and compassionate language, who by this fair exterior awakens the hope of the wretched—but after all confines his bounty to mere words and looks—resembles the fig tree, which the Savior cursed, because it was covered with delusive foliage, yet was destitute of fruit to satisfy the hungry.

7.2. The PROPERTIES of Christian Mercy.

7.2.1. Mercy is supported and directed by the principles of the New Testament, and not merely by the force of natural feeling.

It will be remembered that I am now speaking of 'Christian mercy'—or, in other words, of that compassion which is represented in the Word of God, as the work of the Divine Spirit, which supposes the previous existence of the Christian character, and which is urged by considerations peculiar to the gospel. The renewed mind of a believer is represented, in the figurative language of the Scripture, as the garden of the Lord; and all the holy virtues of sanctification as the fruits and flowers which, by a heavenly agency, have been planted in it. Between these 'holy virtues'—and the 'natural virtues of the unrenewed heart' there is a considerable resemblance, as there is between the wild plants of nature—and plants of the same species when removed to the garden, and placed beneath care and skill. I admit there is much mercy, much amiable compassion, shedding their fragrance and yielding their fruits in the wilderness of corrupt nature; refreshing the weary by the former, and by the latter satisfying the needs of the hungry.

We have sometimes the *melancholy* spectacle to see a man whom a whole village or a town unites to bless, because he has been eyes to the blind, and feet to the lame, and a father to the poor, and has fed the hungry, and clothed the naked, and healed the sick, and caused the widow's heart to sing for joy; to see such a man— because he has not erected his mercy seat, like that in the temple, upon the Rock of God's choice—swept away with the refuse of the earth, and the wreck of nations who know not God. I pretend not to determine what effect 'natural loveliness of disposition' without saving religion may have in lessening the torments of hell, but if there be any truth in the Scripture—it will not elevate to the joys of heaven. A deist, or an atheist, may be of a merciful disposition, but will this save him? One feels a reluctance in applying the denunciatory parts of revealed truth to men, who, though they are apparently destitute of all real religion, possess everything else that can adorn humanity, and render them the blessing of mankind; and yet when so many are perpetually told, and so readily believe the assertion, that 'charity is a passport to the skies', it would be cruel if those who know the reality and consequences of the delusion, were to be silent, and not to declare that—the most amiable and diffusive benevolence, if unaccompanied by the essentials of true religion, will leave a man after all within the flood of divine vengeance, where he will be swallowed up by its approaching tide.

Paul expressly declares that though a man gives all his goods to feed the poor, and has not love—that is, love to God, leading to a proper regard of our fellow-creatures—he is nothing. Many have deluded themselves on this subject by the dreadful perversion of a passage of inspired truth, which utters a sentiment the most remote from that which it has been made to promulgate. "Charity," say these people, "shall cover the multitude of sins." Now, by charity, here, is meant love; and the sentiment contained in the expression is nothing more than that love will conceal with a friendly covering, instead of publishing to the world, a multitude of imperfections in those we regard. This is its true meaning. If it meant that God accepts those people who whose alms-deeds outweigh their crimes—it would justify all the vile and horrid hypocrisy the wicked, for if lesser acts of benevolence will cover lesser sins, there are no vices so flagrant which may not be covered on this principle, by an increase of munificence.

Let it not be said, that the **motive** of a merciful act is of no consequence, provided the compassion is felt, and the relief communicated. I admit that in relation to the object of our mercy, and the interests of society with regard to him, this remark is correct. In reference to these, it is no matter what was the motive which dictated the act; whether the doer of it had the glory of God in view, or whether he was an infidel. But our actions sustain other relations, which make it of infinite and eternal consequence under what motives, and upon what principles, they are performed. The question is, what influence our conduct will have, not upon the comfort of others, but upon our own eternal destiny; not what may be demanded by our fellow-creatures, whose most penetrating discrimination cannot reach the heart—but what may be and is required by that Omniscient Being, to whom the very soul, with all its most secret contents, is an open and legible page. In short, the question is not what constitutes worldly morality, but what is essential to pure Christian religion.

We go on to observe, then, that **true Christian mercy**—that which will be accepted in the sight of God, and receive his smile; that which will ensure his gracious and unmerited reward, and which will have no slight connection with our celestial happiness, **is exercised in designed obedience to God's command, in express imitation of his conduct, and with an earnest desire to promote his glory.** This is the ground on which it is enjoined, "Be merciful, as your Father who is in heaven is merciful." This disposition is cherished by a devout contemplation of that mercy which shines from heaven upon the human race through the cross of our Lord Jesus Christ. With other men, mercy is merely a 'feeling'—with the Christian it is a 'principle'. By them, it is exercised in gratification of their inclination; by the believer, at the dictate of conscience. They think it is kind for one needy creature to compassionate another; in addition to the force of this sentiment, the Christian reasons—that if God has so far pitied him as to deliver his soul from eternal misery, the least spark of gratitude must lead him to relieve the needs of his fellow-creatures. They go no higher than to gratify their own propensities; the Christian desires to honor God. They expect, by deeds of mercy, to merit eternal life; but the Christian depends, amidst the most profuse benevolence, upon the righteousness of Christ.

7.2.2. Christian Mercy displays tenderness of MANNER, in her acts of liberality.

It is akin to that charity which is kind, and resembles that goodness of our heavenly Father, which "gives to all men liberally, and upbraids not." There are many ways of communicating relief to the wretched, but this lovely virtue will choose that which will least oppress the feelings of its object. It will act the part of the tender surgeon, who, in healing the wounds of his patient, will inflict no unnecessary pain. A rough and churlish man, whatever may be his skill, is unfit for the chamber of pain and sickness. Mercy needs a quick, discerning eye, a gentle hand, a tender heart; many of its objects must be dealt with delicately. It is a feminine virtue, and should partake of the softness and mildness of femininity. There should be nothing in our manner unnecessarily to wound the feelings of those whose miseries we wish to relieve; no upbraiding should accompany our beneficence; what we communicate should not appear to be extorted from a reluctant hand; it should not be like the spark smitten from a flint; nor like water squeezed from a sponge; but mercy should drop like balm upon the wounded spirit of the sufferer.

The smallest act of mercy will in every case be doubly sweet when administered with kindness; while the most substantial benevolence, tossed in petulance to the miserable, may aggravate the suffering which it is intended to mitigate. Like Him, who has left us an example, that we should follow his steps, we should be careful not "to break the bruised reed."

7.2.3. Christian mercy adds the greatest COURAGE IN ACTION—to the greatest tenderness of feeling.

There are some who would be thought to possess too much compassion to endure the sight of human woe. They flee the scenes of wretchedness, and never venture down into the dark and gloomy abodes where misery dwells in all its loathsome and repulsive forms. At such sights, their senses are offended, their feelings are shocked, their comforts are interrupted, and they resolve to expose themselves no more to the scene of misery. But this 'sickly sensibility' deserves no higher character than selfishness in disguise, or cowardice—varnished with the tears of mock compassion. What would the miserable do if there were no other pity than this in the world, and no other benefactors than these to be found? Many of the forms of human wretchedness are of the most disgusting nature, and others of the most shocking nature—and every person of feeling would, on every ground but the hope of communicating relief, preserve the greatest distance from them.

But mercy, like the physician, consults not her pleasure, but the calls of duty; and bracing up her nerves, and fortifying herself with motives, and kindling all her courage—flies to the scene of need and suffering. Would you see this virtue in all its sublimity and grandeur, go, not to the study of the sentimentalist, where, weeping over the tale of unreal sorrows, in fancied tenderness of his heart, he hides himself from all the sights and sounds of actual woe, and whence he occasionally sends abroad his alms, without daring to trust himself amidst the living forms of grief; but follow the philanthropist from his home, the resort of plenty, luxury, and elegance—and trace him along the dirty and narrow alley, where the poorest of the poor herd together, amid poverty, and wretchedness, and vice; where there is everything to offend every sense, and some new shape of misery or 'specter of deprivation' crosses his path at every step; where sounds which seem the wailings and blasphemies of the damned, at every step, come across his ear; see this herald of mercy, trembling, yet pressing onward, through all these horrors, to reach a hovel in the center of this earthly hell, where, amidst filth, and poverty, and disease, lies gasping a human being, to whom he is anxious to convey the comforts of one world, and the hopes of another. This is mercy!

Behold the man, whose memory will never perish until the milk of kindness in the bosom of our species be trans-venomed into the poison of asps, and whose name will be heard with transports on the banks of every river, until those rivers shall forget to flow—the immortal Howard, pacing backward and forward over the globe in search of misery, diving into the depths of dungeons, plunging into the infection of hospitals, surveying every building in which society inflicts or hides away sorrow and pain. This is mercy. Behold that heroine of our own days, who, urged by the mighty impulses of her own brave heart (Mother Theresa of Calcutta), in opposition to kind advice, and as it seemed at first with neglect of prudence, but as we see now, under the protection of God, whose messenger she was, ventured within the walls of India, where, in addition to all that could offend the eye, the ear, the touch, the smell—there was everything to shock the moral sense. See this astonishing woman, descending from splendor to place herself amidst scenes of living, crawling filth, and leaving for a season the pure and quiet endearments of her home—to collect around her a band of furies, maddened at once by disease and vice; and all this for the simple purpose of reforming creatures considered by society beyond any hope, and below every effort for their improvement. This is mercy. Go, you soft and sentimental benefactors of the human race, who can weep for wretchedness, but cannot bear to see it; go, look at these sublime and beautiful characters—and learn what mercy is.

7.2.4. To judicious discrimination between true and false misery, Christian mercy unites a propensity to relieve ALL misery, on its own account.

We certainly ought not to allow ourselves to be easily imposed upon by "that cunning craftiness which lies in wait to deceive." An *indiscriminate liberality* supplies a stimulus to vice, is a rewarder to fraud, and afterwards, when deception has been frequently detected, by a powerful reaction it overturns the very throne of mercy itself—for no one is more likely to have his heart steeled against all appeals to his compassion than he who, after a long course of benevolence, discovers that his pity has been often wasted upon pretended distress. But while this discrimination must be exercised, there should be a disposition to relieve to the extent of our ability—**all real misery**.

We can easily conceive, for it is a case of frequent occurrence, that misery may in some instances be attended by circumstances that give it a deep interest, and invest it with a charm of peculiar and resistless fascination. Even the churl, the miser, and the cruel oppressor—have bowed at the feet of afflicted beauty, and allowed themselves for once to be led captive in the fetters of mercy. There is a romantic kind of pity in the world, which silly tales, falling in with mawkish sensibility, have helped to produce and cherish—I mean that disposition which is ever seeking after what it considers interesting objects of compassion. Misery, exhibited naked and alone, as it may be found in every street and every day, has no power to set in motion this spurious passion. The cries of hunger, the groans of sickness, the plaint of woe—return unheeded in sad echoes upon the sufferer's heart, unless the child of romance can discover some moving incentives to give, and which might serve as the basis of some striking and pathetic tale. I call this the mercy, not of the heart, but of the imagination; the compassion of the novelist, of the poet, of the painter, but not of the Christian. It should be recollected that there may be the most deep and entire wretchedness, without either youth, or beauty, or rapid vicissitude, or complicated plot, in the case. It is but seldom that we shall meet with instances of woe so varied and interesting in their details as to form a picture for the pages of a story. If we wait for such scenes to awaken our compassion, the world will die around us, and we shall die in the midst of it—before we have hushed a groan, or wiped away a tear.

7.2.5. Christian Mercy Is characterized by DILIGENCE.

It is said of our Lord, that "he ever went about doing good;" and the history of his life proves the truth of the assertion. Whether in the crowded city, or the retired village; whether in the domestic circle, or the courts of the temple; whether he led the multitude into the wilderness, or met them amidst the social haunts of men—he was ever engaged in acts of compassion, both to the souls and bodies of mankind. His errand to our world was a commission of mercy, and all his actions here an uninterrupted display of pity. We are to find our model in Him who never slept in the cause of human happiness. Diligence characterizes the efforts of the enemies of the human race, and it should surely not be lacking in its friends. The powers of darkness, with an energy of which we can form no adequate conception, are perpetually scattering the seeds of human misery, and causing the thorn, the bramble, and the nettle, to grow with noxious lushness in the path of life. We must oppose energy to energy, and diligence to diligence.

The objects of our pity are every hour passing in crowds, above the need of our efforts, or below the reach of our efforts; rising to heaven, where misery never enters, or sinking to hell, where mercy is never seen. Sin and disease, accidents and injustice, misfortune and death, are every moment busily employed, in extending the range and the reign of misery; and surely mercy should not be tardy or lukewarm. Our compassion should not be fretful or capricious—today all ardor, tomorrow all languor—but steadfast, immoveable, always abounding. Whatever our hand finds to do, we should do it with our might.

7.2.6. Christian Mercy should be attended with SELF-DENIAL.

We are not to offer on her altar the halt, the blind, and the lame, the mere surplus of our comforts, which we deem below our notice. Nor are we to be content with yielding up the surplus of our possessions, which we do not want, and cannot use. We must stand prepared to make sacrifices, and endure hardships. It is shocking to think how little some people will do to relieve the miseries of others. If they can supply the wants of the needy, and alleviate the woes of the afflicted, without going a step out of their way, abridging themselves of a single comfort, or giving up a moment's ease—they feel no objection to do a generous act. But if they must endure the least fatigue, or sacrifice what is in any degree valuable to themselves, tears may flow in torrents, and groans may rise in dismal concert, before they can be excited to deeds of mercy. They will not abridge one of all their luxurious gratifications, although the 'prunings' of almost any of them would be enough to guard the cottage of a poor neighbor from the worst terrors of poverty.

Did the Son of God exhibit a species of compassion which cost him nothing? Did he, without effort and without humiliation, give us the mere surplus of his riches, the redundance of his glory? Did he only speak from the throne of his majesty, or dispatch a company of angels from the countless multitudes ministering around his feet, to bring us tidings of mercy, expressions of his good will? Altogether the opposite! "You know the grace of our Lord Jesus Christ, who though he was rich, yet for our sakes became poor, that we, through his poverty, might become rich." The measure of his self-denial was the difference between his throne of glory—and his cross. Can that man, who will not make the smallest sacrifice in mercy's cause, persuade himself that he is a disciple of this merciful, self-denying Redeemer?

7.2.7. Christian mercy is not discouraged by the ingratitude or the opposition which may be manifested by those whom it relieves.

That man has calculated too highly upon human virtue who believes that benevolence will always be rewarded by the gratitude of those whose needs are supplied, and whose sorrows are mitigated, by its exertions. It is too common a fault of mankind—first to mistake, and then to forget, their benefactors. Mercy is not always received with the promptitude with which it is offered. Some are too proud to be dependent, and turn with scorn from the hand that would lift them into comfort; others sullenly receive the assistance as their due, and stoop not to thank the generosity to which they are indebted.

It is not thus with all. Tears of gratitude often repay the philanthropist with a reward, compared with which the gems of India are but as dust. If, however, we would do good, we must do it looking only to the smile of conscience, and of God, for our remuneration. It is delightful to behold poverty and need, and disease and sorrow, disappearing before us in the path of mercy, although we may see ingratitude filling their place. We have still the comfort of reflecting, that notwithstanding we have done our duty—and the 'sum of human wretchedness' is less. In this respect, also, we may be instructed by the history of our divine Savior. He flew to our world on the wings of mercy, he was himself incarnate love, truth dwelt on his lips, compassion reigned in his heart; wherever he directed his course the miseries of multitudes vanished before the miracles of his grace—and salvation followed his footsteps. He was the teacher who instructed their minds, the benefactor who satisfied their hunger, the physician who healed their disorders, the deliverer who would have saved their souls; yet, for all this, he was maligned, calumniated, hated, persecuted, murdered! And shall we expect to find the path of benevolence like one of the walks of paradise, where the serpent was harmless beneath the flowers? If we do, we shall soon discover our mistake.

7.3.　The OBJECTS of Christian Mercy.

And I am sure no one will accuse me of degrading the subject, if, for a few moments, I urge the claims of that large portion of the **animate creation** to which Providence has denied the power of pleading its own cause. Oh! there is a depth of cowardice, cruelty, and injustice in inflicting misery upon an irrational brute,

deprived of all means of resistance and all power of complaint, except by its quivering flesh and screaming cries, for which language is too feeble to furnish execrations sufficiently emphatic. Let me never fall into the hands, or be at the mercy of that man, who, whatever may be his pretensions or his character, would wantonly inflict a pang on the least and lowest insect in the scale of life. Man is, or ought to be, the guardian of the rights of the irrational creation; but, lest he should be unfaithful to his trust, the great God has interposed his authority, and raised a causeless injury of any of his creatures into a crime against their Almighty Creator. Remember, then, that "a merciful man is merciful to his animal."
But the chief object of mercy—is MAN.

7.3.1. Christian Mercy Regards Man's TEMPORAL wants and woes.

Innumerable are "the ills which flesh is heir to" in this valley of tears. Poverty, sickness, hunger, nakedness, toil—all, like roots of bitterness, spring up along the road which conducts us to the grave. And all, the merciful man, to the utmost of his power, will endeavor to repress or eradicate. He will not hide himself from such sorrows. His own comforts will remind him of the necessities of others. A sense of the woes by which he is surrounded, will reach him at the center of that wide circle of plenty within which he dwells, and will not allow him to enjoy what Providence has given him, until, with no scanty hand, he has administered to their relief. He will remember that others are men of like passions with himself, and that if with so many comforts to sweeten the cup of life, he so often tastes the wormwood and the gall—their portion must be wretched indeed, to whom, but for the aid of mercy, the draught must be unmingled bitterness.

It has been adopted as a maxim by some good, but mistaken people, that as "the children of the world" devote all their charity to the temporal wants of mankind, "the children of light "should exclusively employ theirs for the spiritual interests of the human race. This appears to me a most erroneous sentiment, and highly derogatory to the honor of religion. We are "to let our light so shine before men, that they, seeing our good works, may glorify God, our heavenly Father." One way of exhibiting the splendor of this holy light, is by excelling in those virtues, the excellences of which are perceived, and the obligations of which are felt, by the people of the world. Zeal for the diffusion of the gospel is, by many, considered only as fanaticism. But mercy to temporal needs, is acknowledged by all to be a necessary Christian virtue. Besides, our motives will be mistaken if we abandon the temporal miseries of mankind; for men will be at a loss to conceive how they can have mercy for the soul—who appear to have none for the body; and how they can feel compassion for strangers whom they have not seen—who are destitute of it towards their neighbors whom they have seen. In the absence of mercy for the temporal miseries of mankind—all our solicitude for their spiritual interests will be resolved into disgusting hypocrisy, which, under pretense of compassion, is carrying on the purposes of mere sectarianism. Our Redeemer's identifying character is the Savior of souls; but how diligent he was in relieving temporal needs, let the history of his life declare.

7.3.2. Christian Mercy extends its regard to the SPIRITUAL miseries of mankind.

The man who believes the Gospel realizes that the whole human race in a state of sin and ruin; suffering all the consequences of sin in this world—and exposed to the bitter pains of eternal death in the world to come. He is convinced that without a fitness for the pure and spiritual joys of heaven, not one individual of all the millions who are continually passing into eternity, can ascend to the realms of glory and felicity. They appear, in his eyes, to be actually perishing, and hence he is filled with the tenderest concern, and affected with the deepest sorrow. In his estimation, the most agonizing diseases, the most pinching poverty, the greatest deprivation, and the heaviest cares—are as nothing, compared with those miseries which sin has brought upon the deathless soul. With all the compassion which he feels for the body, he cannot forget, that if it were not relieved, the grave would soon terminate its woes; but that the soul, if not saved, would become immortal in its suffering and wretchedness.

This makes him not only willing, but anxious to support every scheme, which has for its object to extend the light of divine truth to those who sit in darkness and the region of the shadow of death. Often he surveys, from his own happy elevation on the hill of Zion, the countless millions that crowd the realms of Paganism and Islamism, until his heart yearning with compassion, dictates to his tongue the prayer of the Psalmist, "God be merciful unto us and bless us, that your way may be known on earth, your saving health among all nations." Nor is he content with expressing his mercy by prayers. He cannot withhold his property, while every breeze and every wave that touches upon our shore wafts to it from the dark places of the earth that heart-rending petition, "Come over and help us!"

Yes, 'mercy to the soul' is the 'soul of mercy'. This is its sublimest, its mightiest effort. It supplies needs, and alleviates woes, which would otherwise be eternal. Its provisions and outcomes will be everlasting, and the grandeur of its results be seen infinite ages after the hospital, the dispensary, and the alms-house shall have sent forth their last stream of healing. Mercy to the soul raises its subject into the nearest resemblance of Yahweh. It is, in fact, "to have fellowship with the Father and with his Son Jesus Christ." The human spirit seems to occupy the center of the divine government, around which the plans and purposes of Deity are perpetually revolving; and the chief end of all their mighty movements is to glorify God in the salvation of man. Who, then, would exclude the soul from the sphere of his compassion? Let us not forget to do good in relieving the temporal needs of our fellow-creatures, but in the exercise of a still holier and loftier ambition, let us aim at the honor of saving the soul. An infinitely richer and more lasting renown will follow such an achievement than the civic crown awarded by the Roman Senate to him who saved the life of a citizen on the field of battle.

7.3.3. Christian Mercy is Connected to Numerous BLESSINGS

"Blessed are the merciful—for they shall obtain mercy." If we considered this language as meaning no more than that the compassionate should, in their necessities, be the objects of pity to their fellow-creatures, we would assert no more than experience proves to be true. Who is so likely to receive the kind and merciful attentions of others, as he who in the days of his prosperity was a fountain of comfort to them? The public will hasten to such a man in the time of his distress, and attempt to discharge the obligations which he had conferred by his liberality. The tide of mercy which had flowed from his heart will return to him again, convincing him that "in such measure as we give to others, it shall be given back to us." When we consider the vicissitudes of this changing world, and think how speedily we may be reduced to the circumstances of those who now depend for relief upon our benevolence, we surely ought to find in such a reflection no feeble inducement to the exercise of mercy. Never can the denial of pity affect the sufferer's heart with such exquisitely painful emotions—as when it seems to come in the way of severe, but righteous retribution, and reminds him of the hour when he closed his own ear to the tale of another's woe.

But the text has a higher meaning, and expresses a far richer and more comprehensive beatitude than this. **They who show mercy to others upon Christian principles, shall themselves obtain mercy from God.** Here it will be necessary for me to state a distinction which is something more than merely a difference in words; I mean the distinction between the 'meritorious cause' of a blessing, and an indispensable prerequisite to its possession. Anyone who has favors to distribute, may require as absolutely essential from everyone who would enjoy them, the performance of a condition which could in no sense be considered as a meritorious cause of the desired favor, because not at all equivalent to it. In this sense, **a merciful disposition to our fellow-creatures is the stipulated condition of our obtaining mercy from God—a prerequisite, but not the cause.** It is not that for the sake of which we obtain mercy, but without which, God's mercy will be denied us. It bears the same relation to eternal happiness as holiness does (of which it is, indeed, a part); "without which no man shall see the Lord." The very mode of expression here employed utterly precludes the idea of pity to our fellow-creatures being the meritorious cause of the divine favor. It is said they shall obtain mercy, which would be a most inappropriate term in the case of merit.

That mercy which God exercises towards man, essentially includes the idea of *guilt* on the part of the latter. It is the compassion, not merely of the benefactor towards simple misery, but of a ruler towards that wretchedness which is the consequence of *crime*. Hence, when it is said, we shall obtain mercy—the possibility of merit is excluded. Merit appeals not to mercy, but to justice. If it is admitted that we have all deserved death by our sins, it is confessed that none of us can become entitled to life by any part of our conduct, since it is impossible for the same being to *merit* both punishment and pardon; indeed, the very idea of our 'meriting pardon' is an absurdity. No! If any sinner is saved, it must be by grace through faith. The most diffusive compassion, united with the most exemplary charity, forms no ground on which a transgressor can rest his hope of pardoning mercy.

"Believe on the Lord Jesus Christ and you shall be saved" is the language of the gospel. This faith, however, produces suitable **fruits**, and one of its inseparable effects is a merciful disposition. Without this there can be no genuine belief of the gospel; where this exists, and compassion is exercised in obedience to the divine Word, in conformity to the divine example, and with a view to the divine glory, there shall the promise of the text be fulfilled—God will blot out the transgressions of such a man, restore him to his favor, pity him in all his distresses, and finally cause his miseries to end in that state where "he will wipe away all tears from their eyes, and there shall be no more death, neither sorrow nor crying, neither shall there be any more pain, for the former things are passed away."

Without 'mercy to others' we have no more reason to expect it from God, than we have to hope for an entrance into heaven without that holiness which is its only preparative. While, on the other hand, in proportion as this disposition of 'mercy to others' prevails in the heart, we have at least one **evidence** of having obtained God's saving mercy. But by the aid of what rhetoric, sophistry, or delusion which the deceitfulness of the human heart may supply, can that man persuade himself that he has received grace from God, who knows, if he knows anything of himself, that 'pity' and 'mercy' is a stranger to his character? A lack of Christian mercy is a no less damning mark upon the soul than a lack of purity or honesty. Let such an unfeeling creature tremble, for he is hastening to take his station before a throne where he shall find judgment, but no mercy!

## 7.4.	The CULTIVATION and the PRACTICE of Christian mercy.

7.4.1. There is the Need to Cultivate and Practice Mercy from the Misery in the Word

By a figure of speech, which is by no means too strong, our present state of existence is said to be a "valley of tears," in which "man is born to trouble as the sparks fly upward." From the hour when our first parents ate the forbidden fruit, they and their offspring have sadly possessed the knowledge of evil. The deep groan with which the great bard represents nature to have marked the perpetration of that awful deed, has been so protracted and so echoed, that it may be justly said, "the whole creation groans, and travails in pain together until now." The world is full of misery of one kind and another. Poverty, sickness, disease, toil, disappointment, and innumerable other causes of distress, are perpetually at work in destroying the comforts of mankind, and embittering the cup of human life. Could we from some upper region in the air, with powers of vision strengthened for the task, look down upon every scene of suffering but in one populous town; could we penetrate into every chamber of sickness, every hovel of poverty, every scene of dreadful foreboding, heart-withering care, and deep despondency; could we see at one glance every widow, every orphan, every fatherless babe, and all the tears they shed at the remembrance of their loss; could we behold all the ignorance and vice to be found within this town, and the souls there perishing in sin; could all the sounds of woe which, from only such a small portion of our race are perpetually rising, to expire unheeded by man on the gales of the wind, enter at once into our ear, surely, surely we should descend from our elevation determined "to sell all our goods and give to the poor."

But though we see it not, a 'mass of misery' does exist in that town—of which we can form no adequate idea. We look upon the 'external show of human life' as the attendants at a theater do upon a comedy—where the brilliant lights, the picturesque scenes, the seeming gaiety of the performers—exclude all ideas of sadness. To form an accurate idea of the real condition of the actors, we would have follow them to the miserable garrets where they are hourly struggling with poverty and care, where, throwing aside the 'pretend characters' assumed for the hour, and losing the smiles put on for the occasion, we would find them most forlorn and miserable.

So if we go behind the scenes of this life's drama, we shall find an internal world of distress—which meets not the eye in public. And can we remain cold and unfeeling, inactive and illiberal—amidst universal misery? Shall we give ourselves up to luxurious enjoyment, while the groans of creation are heard all around us? Shall the lament of human woe be but as the serenade of our selfish gratification? Shall the tear fall perpetually with less power of impression on our spirits, than the dropping of water upon a rock? Shall human cries move us less than the sighing of the wind does the mountain oak? Let us all become philanthropists upon a scale proportioned to our circumstances! Let us all be actuated by a noble, merciful ambition to leave the world holier and happier than we found it! There is much for us all to do; and after we have all done our uttermost, much will remain undone.

7.4.2. You Have Power to alleviate Human Misery.

Most men underrate their means of doing good. Few are aware of the full extent of their ability to bless others. It may be safely affirmed that there is not one rational being so sunk in poverty, or so circumscribed in influence, as to be deprived of all opportunity of diminishing the sum of human wretchedness. It is to be apprehended that a mistake on this subject prevents many from exerting themselves as they should do in the cause of humanity. They suppose that philanthropy requires, in every case, a large capital of wealth, influence, and talent. Nothing is more erroneous! It is true, that the larger the stock of those things which a man possesses, the more good he can do. But to imagine that we must be either rich, or great, or learned, in order to be a blessing to others, is a mistake which robs us of much pleasure, and society of much assistance. Let there be only the assiduous cultivation of a merciful disposition, coupled with a determination to exercise it to the uttermost, and it is astonishing to find how many channels will open through which to pour the streams of benevolence. If we have not property of our own, we may be able to exert our influence over those who have it; and we may become the almoners of those who have no leisure or inclination to distribute their own benefactions.

Each of us should enquire in what particular way he can be most useful to the interests and comforts of mankind. Our situation and circumstances vary so much, that the same schemes of usefulness do not adapt themselves with equal facility to all. We should study our temper, fortune, talents, and neighborhood, with a view to ascertain whether there is in either of these any peculiarity which seems to mark us out more for one sphere of action than another; and it should never be forgotten by those who have large means of usefulness, that exertion is binding on them in exact proportion to the extent of their ability.

The responsibility attaching to wealth seems to be but imperfectly understood after all that has been said or written on the subject. It should ever be borne in mind that the exercise of mercy and charity is represented by our Lord in his description of the judgment day, as one of the principal topics of scrutiny in that season of final retribution. What a spectacle of horror and amazement will the rich man then present, who lavished in selfish extravagance that princely fortune which was entrusted to him for the benefit of society. Let such men read the parable of Dives and Lazarus; its salutary and impressive warnings were delivered expressly for them.

Wealth considered as a means of sensual gratification, ranks but one step above the acorns of the swine; while as a means of relieving misery, it opens sources of felicity, lofty and sublime as the joy of angels. It is a transporting picture which the fancy presents to the soul, by portraying what the world would be if every rich man were a benefactor; if all our wealthy tradesmen, gentry, and nobility, were to employ a suitable proportion of their property in lessening human misery, and increasing human happiness. But long, we fear, it will be before such a picture will be realized.

7.4.3. There is HAPPINESS attending upon a merciful spirit.

Duty and personal interest are in every case inseparably connected, but never more obviously than in this. Of mercy may be strictly said, what is affirmed of piety in general, "her commands are not grievous, but joyous, and in keeping of them there is great reward." It is true that a sympathizing spirit, in some measure, makes the sorrows of others its own, but its tears, like a shower in summer, produce a refreshing atmosphere, and are far more pleasant than that cold stiffness and frosty hardness which prevail in the bosom of the unmerciful man. Think with what emotions Howard must have reposed on his pillow, after a day spent in carrying the cup of mercy into dungeons, as in his dreams he still beheld the captives quaffing the delicious draught. Think what must have been the sublime bliss of the liberator of Africa, on that solemnly delightful evening, when, after smiting for twenty years on the fetters of slavery, he saw them yield at last to his toilsome and patient exertions; and to the vision which had so often in imploring attitude exclaimed, "Come over and help us," he could at length reply, "Your chains are broken; Africa be free." And even in lesser instances of mercy, there is a luxury which holy generous minds alone can know, and with which all the gratifications of vanity, and the pleasures of sense, cannot be brought into comparison. God is the happiest of beings, because he is the most benevolent. It is expressly said, that "he delights in mercy." We can form no idea of the manner in which the Deity is susceptible of pleasure; it is enough for us to know, that in whatever manner this delight is experienced, it arises from the exercise of mercy; and surely if it administers pleasure to him who sits on the eternal throne, it might be expected to afford some of the purest bliss that mortals know on earth.

Let any man be able to appropriate to himself the language of Job, and his bosom will be conscious of a bliss which a seraph must almost feel inclined to envy, "When they heard me, they blessed me, and when they saw me, they spoke well of me. For I rescued the poor man who cried out for help, and the fatherless child who had no one to support him. The dying man blessed me, and I made the widow's heart rejoice. I clothed myself in righteousness, and it enveloped me; my just decisions were like a robe and a turban. I was eyes to the blind and feet to the lame. I was a father to the needy, and I examined the case of the stranger. (Job 29:11-16)

7.4.4. Remember your own dependence on Divine mercy, both for all the comforts of this life, and all the blessings of the life which is to come.

It is, indeed, an impressive consideration, eminently calculated on the one hand to encourage our hopes, but certainly on the other to awaken our alarm—that we are all most entirely at the mercy of God. Having sinned against his law we have forfeited our souls to his justice, and depend for happiness on that grace which he is under no other obligation to exercise, than that which he has imposed upon himself, by his own promise. If we are ever saved at all, it must be by an act of goodness still more unmerited than that which we should perform, were we to bestow a favor upon the man who had done his uttermost to injure us. God could utterly destroy us, and from the very ruins of our eternal state, raise a monument to the praise of his justice. The smoke of our torment ascending up forever and ever, would cast no reflection upon the equity of his proceeding, or throw any shadow upon the perfection of his administration.

"God be merciful to me a sinner," is the humble petition which best suits our character in every approach to his throne. Upon that mercy we are every hour living. It is this mercy which keeps us from dropping into the pit, whence there is no redemption; this which gives us every comfort we enjoy on earth; this which opens to us the prospect of eternal glory. And shall we, who owe everything we possess, everything we hope for, to the unmerited grace of God, deny the exercise of mercy to our fellow-creatures? Shall we, who must perish eternally, unless God be full of compassion towards us—be lacking in pity towards those who are in any measure dependent for their comfort on us? Where is the heart that can resist the force of these considerations? Let us yield ourselves up to their influence, and convince the world that the wisdom which descends from above, is indeed what the Scriptures declare it to be, "full of mercy and good fruits."

Be merciful, therefore, in every other case of human misery, to the extent of your ability. Many will bless you for your benevolence. And even if gratitude had left the earth, your witness is in heaven, and your reward is on high. A day is approaching when, not a cup of cold water administered to the parched lips of wretchedness, in obedience to the authority, and in imitation of the mercy of God, shall be either forgotten, or overlooked, by him who has the destiny of man at his disposal. To the solemnities and decisions of that day I refer you!

CHAPTER EIGHT

SOME THINGS TO KEEP IN MIND ABOUT THE WORK OF MERCY IN THE LIFE OF THE BELIEVER

8.1.   Mercy is for everyone.

One of the greatest misconceptions of my early years as a Catholic was that Catholicism is a two-track system. Lay people just need to worry about keeping the precepts of the church and the Ten Commandments. The Sermon on the Mount and real holiness is the territory of those called to priesthood and religious life. Knowing that this misconception was pervasive, the Second Vatican Council affirmed in its Dogmatic Constitution on the Church that the call to true holiness is absolutely universal (*Lumen Gentium*, Chap V). And holiness means love, and love means mercy. Therefore, works of mercy can't just be relegated to those who belong to the social justice committee or the Missionaries of Charity. Everyone, without exception, is called to the work of mercy.

8.2.   Mercy relieves suffering, and there are different kinds of suffering.

I once heard a Catholic in France offer a striking petition in the prayer of the Faithful: "let us pray for all those suffering from the pain of not knowing the love of God." The lack of bodily necessities certainly causes great distress. But so does lack of the things of the spirit. It is important to keep in mind that the Church enumerates not only corporal works of mercy but spiritual works of mercy as well, and that the latter actually have a certain preeminence. Perhaps not all are quite ready to instruct the ignorant or admonish sinners. But at least one of the spiritual works of mercy is something that virtually all of us can do, regardless of our location or state of health: interceding for the living and the dead. Indeed this is the work of mercy performed by the glorified saints in heaven.

8.3. Mercy begins at Home.

That Angel of Mercy, Blessed Mother Teresa of Calcutta, was often approached by people who were moved to want to share in her apostolate to the poorest of the poor. Her advice was often "go home and love your own family". If we open our eyes there are people all around us who are lonely, sick, overworked, and troubled. They very much need our compassion and attention. This is where we must start. "If any one does not provide for his relatives, and especially for his own family, he has disowned the faith and is worse than an unbeliever." (I Timothy 5:8).

8.4. Mercy can't end at Home

The story of the Good Samaritan is striking for a number of reasons, not the least of which is the fact that the hero of the story has no natural bond with the victim. Jews and Samaritans actually had great antipathy for each other. So we can't restrict our works of mercy to family, friends, and those who belong to our Church or political party. As Jesus tells us in the Sermon on the Mount, our works of mercy must extend even to our enemies.

8.5. Mercy is not always Convenient.

There are times that works of mercy can be planned and fit in an orderly way into our schedule. But suffering and crisis are often unpredictable. And responding to them can often be very inconvenient. The Good Samaritan took a lot of time and went through no small expense to make sure the victim in the story was provided for. He was probably late for an appointment as a result.

8.6. Charity is not the same as Social Work.

While people often refer to anything that benefits the disadvantaged as "charity," the word actually means divine, supernatural love. It is action that springs from the love of God which has been poured into our hearts by the Holy Spirit (Romans 5:5) and must involve not just giving things but giving our ourselves. We must see God's image and likeness in the person that benefits from our act and love that person for God's sake. There is nothing wrong with making a year-end charitable gift, but if this is to be a true work of mercy, the motivation must be deeper than the wish for a tax write-off. For St. Francis and Mother Teresa, serving the poorest of the poor was serving Jesus Himself (Matthew 25:34ff). The work of mercy can and should be a deeply spiritual encounter.

8.7. Mercy is Never Condescending.

The goal of the Ancient Enemy of mankind is to use suffering to rob those made in God's image of their human dignity. Our goal in the work of mercy is always to restore that dignity and honor it. "Charity" that belittles the recipient is never true mercy. It may relieve some bodily suffering but only causes a deeper suffering of alienation and humiliation. The Divine Word emptied himself of glory and stood shoulder to shoulder with us. The one giving mercy cannot look down on the recipient of mercy. In fact the merciful humbly understand that they always receive as much or more as they give when they work to alleviate the suffering of the needy.

Blessed John Paul II wrote an Encyclical on God the Father near the beginning of His Pontificate. With all the possible descriptions and titles for God used in Scripture and Tradition, what was he to title such an encyclical? The answer for him was simple: "Rich in Mercy" (Eph 2:4) God is preeminently the Father of Mercies and the God of all Consolation (2 Corinthians 1:3). The way we can be recognized as his authentic offspring is by living a lifestyle of mercy. It is interesting that in the only description of the last judgment in the Bible, salvation or damnation hangs not on how much religious art people have in their houses or how many Masses they've attended, but how they've treated the least of Jesus' needy brothers and sisters.

CHAPTER NINE

WORKS OF MERCY

Works of mercy can be directed not only toward the needs of the body, but the needs of the soul as well. Indeed, the most serious form of poverty of all can be the *poverty of the spirit*, not only because it drains life of all energy, joy, and sense of purpose, but also because it is the one kind of poverty that can last forever. The evangelist Billy Graham tells the story of a private dinner he shared with one of the wealthiest men in the United States. During the meal the man confessed that despite having every good thing money could buy, he was miserable beyond words. The lesson: money cannot buy happiness. It's a cliché, but it's true. Clearly, this wealthy gentleman suffered from moral poverty. Indeed, the human spirit longs for the nourishment of truth, goodness, and beauty if it is to be healthy and strong and if it is to grow in sanctification and be prepared for the life to come.

Let us now sum up the pattern of life to which our Lord is calling us. Centered on the Merciful Heart of Jesus, whose love is poured into our hearts especially through prayer and the Eucharist, we are to let His merciful love flow through our hearts toward anyone in need whom we meet along life's way. One person who taught this way of life clearly, and who manifested it so beautifully in her apostolate, was Bl. Mother Teresa of Calcutta. She used to say that there are two kinds of "Real Presence" of our Lord in this world: the Lord's Real Presence in the Blessed Sacrament, where He fills us with His light, His life, and His love, and our Lord's real presence in the poor, both in those materially poor and those spiritually poor, where He is waiting for us to give Him back His light, His life, and His love. Living on the Bread of Life, we *receive* our Savior's merciful love; sharing our bread with those who hunger physically and spiritually, we *return* that love back to Him, giving His compassionate Heart solace and joy.

Mother Teresa dedicated her life to picking up the poor and the suffering from the streets of Calcutta and other major cities in India and providing for them the most basic necessities: food, shelter, a blanket, and a bit of human warmth and kindness. Many were desperately sick with incurable illnesses, but it made no difference to Mother Teresa and her Sisters of Charity. They were committed to loving the poor as "Jesus in disguise," so to speak. The sisters saw the Lord as truly present in all who suffer.

The Catholic Church has traditionally encouraged her children to understand the practice of merciful love by dividing the works of mercy into two kinds: corporal (that is, bodily) and spiritual. What we see in the life of Mother Teresa is a shining example of a life dedicated especially to practicing the corporal works of mercy.

9.1. Corporal Works of Mercy

(1) Feed the hungry.
(2) Give drink to the thirsty.
(3) Clothe the naked.
(4) Shelter the homeless.
(5) Visit those in prison.
(6) Comfort the sick.
(7) Bury the dead.

Perhaps your first reaction upon reading this traditional list might be, "This list is a bit out of date. After all, when do we ever have the opportunity in the modern world to 'give drink to the thirsty' or to 'clothe the naked'? And who in their right mind would fail to bury their loved ones these days!" Don't be too hasty, however, in dismissing the usefulness of this old list of the corporal works of mercy. It may be more helpful than you think in challenging us to discern new ways that our merciful Savior is calling us to follow Him.

Moreover, as we shall see, in the practice of each of the corporal works of mercy there is both a *personal* and a wider *social* dimension, and a true disciple of Jesus Christ will not want to neglect either one. Our merciful Savior, after all, is the true and rightful "Lord" of all creation, and that includes every aspect of human life: personal life, married and family life, ecclesiastical life, and even the social, economic and political dimensions of our lives. Do not be afraid of seeking our Lord's will in the latter areas: it does not necessarily mean we must engage in "partisan politics," but we are sometimes called to struggle against extreme and manifest social evils that degrade the human person, such as racism, poverty, tyranny, or violations of the fundamental human right to life, such as abortion and euthanasia. Accepting Jesus as our Lord and Savior includes rejecting everything incompatible with His reign of compassion and merciful love.

9.1.1. Feed the Hungry and Give Drink to the Thirsty

On the surface at least, feeding the hungry seems fairly straightforward. We can help the hungry in simple ways: for example, by making donations to the local food bank or, if we have the time, by helping at a local soup kitchen for the homeless. Moreover, unlike Christians in the ancient and medieval world (when this list of corporal works of mercy was first compiled), we can take the time to educate ourselves about the problem of hunger in the world, and we can use our voices and our votes to petition and pressure our politicians to make the fight against world hunger a higher priority for our government.

Giving drink to the thirsty can also be accomplished through our role as voters: for example, by supporting clean water policies to ensure that there will be clean water for future generations to drink. Meanwhile, right in our own homes we can make our contributions to the effort to preserve clean, fresh water: for example, by using environmentally friendly laundry detergents or by trying to be moderate in the amount of water we put on our lawns.

Typhoid and other diseases were rampant in part related to a lack of fresh drinking water in developing countries.

9.1.2. Clothe the Naked and Shelter the Homeless

We can practice these works of mercy by using, once again, our votes: this time to support policies of the local and national governments that lead to the creation of jobs and that provide an adequate "safety net" for the poor and the homeless. There is room for honest disagreement among Catholics, of course, as to what kinds of governmental policies will most effectively achieve those goals, but our universal concern for the plight of the poor must be acknowledged as a genuine priority. The *Catechism of the Catholic Church* teaches: "[Human] misery elicited the compassion of Christ the Savior ... Hence, those who are oppressed by poverty are the object of a *preferential love* on the part of the Church" (2448).

There are also well-established groups that specialize in relieving the problem of homelessness. Supporting their work is almost always a great way to practice these works of mercy. For example, Habitat for Humanity enables volunteers to actually lend a hand in building brand-new homes for the poor and underprivileged. If you have ever seen their volunteers in action, it is reminiscent of the old prairie tradition of a "barn raising," during which the whole local community would come together to help a farmer who needed a new barn, and they would put it up in a single day! Many of the homeless people in urban areas are young people — often runaways from difficult family situations — kids who live on the streets who often sink into the mire of the drug and prostitution culture. Remember that our Lord himself started His life as a homeless child--born in a manger because there was no room at the inn--and often, throughout His ministry, He had nowhere to lay His head. He must have a special compassion for those who have had to share so closely in His experience of periodic homelessness.

As for "clothing the naked," you can always go through your closets and find garments to donate to the needy. Local thrift shops would be happy to make them available to the needy at a low cost (and often those thrift shops are selling their items to raise money for other good causes, too, such as a local hospital or hospice).

Finally, bear in mind that those of you who are working hard each day to earn the money to provide food and drink, clothing and shelter for your own families, and those of you who cook and clean at home, are already practicing these corporal works of mercy, at least *outwardly*. Why not practice them *inwardly* now as well, from the heart, not grudgingly or merely out of routine, but with compassion and love for your spouse and children, doing all to the glory of God and giving thanks to God the Father for providing for all your needs (see I Cor. 10:31, Col. 3:17). In this way, as St. Paul wrote, the simplest daily chore becomes "a living sacrifice, holy and acceptable to God," a true "spiritual worship" (Rom 12:1).

9.1.3. Visit those in Prison, Comfort the Sick

Visiting those in prison certainly does not mean being "soft on crime." On the contrary, there are some crimes so horrible that their perpetrators must be completely and irrevocably quarantined, put behind bars for a long time or even for life, for the protection of society and to deter other criminals from daring to commit such evil acts in the future. With some violent criminals, society has little choice but to "lock them up and throw away the key."

Throw away the key, indeed — but not the *person*. Punishment deters and quarantines and gives the criminal the opportunity to do penance, but friendship and prayer have the capacity to reform and to heal. A true work of mercy is done by Christians who befriend those in correctional institutions in the name of Jesus Christ, thereby affirming their human dignity as persons made in God's image.

For example, Charles Colson, the former Watergate conspirator, was converted to the Christian faith while serving time in prison. Now he runs a major prison outreach ministry. Eucharistic Apostles of The Divine Mercy cenacles sometimes take on the work of visiting those behind bars and starting EADM cenacles in their local correctional institutions. Such cenacles help enable prisoners to study the *Diary of St. Faustina*, the Scriptures, and the *Catechism*, and grow in their knowledge and love of the Lord. In short, needy persons on our "doorstep" that we are not supposed to "step over" (i.e., neglect; see Lk. 16: 19-20) can sometimes be those in the prison nearby.

The sixth corporal work of mercy is to comfort the sick. At the Shrine of The Divine Mercy in Bulaclan, the Philippines, for example, there is a medical clinic open each week. Qualified doctors and nurses donate their services to provide free medical care for those who cannot afford any. Millions of people cannot afford to purchase medical care. An adequate medical safety net for the poor is still badly needed.

Of course, there are some people who are "sick" not from physical illness but from social isolation. One thinks especially of the elderly in our communities who, whether at home or in long-term care facilities, live in geographical isolation from their loved ones. "Visiting the sick" in our world can mean reaching out to the friendless in our local nursing homes: those who are "sick at heart" from being lonely and forgotten and who are regularly deprived of the basic human need called "friendship." This corporal work of mercy is relatively easy to do. It takes no extensive background reading in economics and no training in political activism to accomplish. The socially isolated elderly are usually not far away. They often live just around the corner from us, or they are members of our own parish. Ask your parish priest to direct you toward those who need visiting in the parish. Most of all, do not forget that some of them may even be members of your own family, relatives too much overlooked and too often forgotten.

Visiting the housebound elderly and the chronically and terminally ill is no easy task. Trying to do it on a regular basis can take us right out of our "comfort zones" because it confronts us with real human lives for which, in earthly terms, there seems to be so little hope. Such people often live in squalor and with the constant stench of sickness or the wince of chronic pain. But our mere presence, as someone willing to be a friend and a listening ear, can mean much more to them than we can imagine, and along the way they will be giving a precious gift to us as well: the gift of growth in the virtue of compassion.

9.1.4. Bury the Dead

No doubt most of us make sure that our relatives and friends have a proper funeral service. But we also need to be aware of the needs of those who are grieving: struggling to "bury their dead" emotionally. Grieving can be a long and arduous process; shedding tears at a funeral rarely completes it. We need to help one another to truly bury our lost loved ones by letting go of them, entrusting them to the hands of our merciful Creator and Savior. That takes friendship — a patient friendship that keeps on visiting the bereaved, keeps on helping them dry their tears, even when the grieving process takes many months or even years. This is a precious work of mercy: to help one another emotionally "bury the dead," entrusting them finally to the merciful Heart of the Redeemer.

In this regard there is something very powerful about the Catholic Tradition of offering Masses for the eternal repose of souls. Contact your parish priest to arrange this for your own departed loved one or for that of a friend or relative.

When we come to the Holy Eucharist, we are actually closer to the faithful departed than at any other time in our lives. After all, whether in purgatory or in heaven, they are in the nearer presence of Jesus Christ, who is also uniquely present to us here on earth in the Blessed Sacrament. To be at "Holy Communion" with Him, therefore, is to be gathered up in a mysterious way into the whole "Communion of Saints" in this life and the life to come. Thus, we can make every Holy Eucharist a time of prayer for departed loved ones and encourage others to do the same.

At this point, after reading about all seven of the corporal works, some readers may be thinking, "It all sounds inspiring in principle, but what can I possibly do? I am already so weighed down with my own issues and responsibilities. I cannot possibly take on any more burdens. I cannot possibly do all these things you suggest!" Of course you can't, and no one is asking you to do so. Not *all* these things. Perhaps just two or three, as you have the opportunity. To accept the challenge of being a true disciple of Jesus Christ, however, means making yourself available to whatever our Lord might call you to do in His service. It means opening your eyes, opening your hearts, and serving His children. It's our duty. Even for those who, through circumstances beyond their control, cannot do much more than they are doing now, they can always pray for those who are doing works of mercy. Pray for those in prison ministry and those advocating for the needs of the poor. Most of all, pray for those struggling to provide food and clothing, shelter and health care for their own families. Whether by deed, word, or prayer, it is always possible for us to practice these basic corporal woks of mercy.

9.2. Spiritual Works of Mercy

(1) Admonish sinners.
(2) Instruct the uninformed.
(3) Counsel the doubtful.
(4) Comfort the sorrowful.
(5) Be patient with those in error.
(6) Forgive offenses.
(7) Pray for the living and the dead.

9.2.1. Admonish Sinners

This work of mercy — "tough love," you could call it — is one of the hardest to practice in the western world today. Why? Because we live in the "I'm-OK-you're-OK" culture. As such, *I* have my own personal set of values, and *you* have your own personal set of values, and we are each free to practice those values to our heart's content just as long as we do not do grievous bodily harm to others in the process (although that limitation is waived when the "others" in question are unborn children, the chronically ill, and elderly).

If you really want to be unpopular — indeed, if you really want to risk getting a punch in the nose — try admonishing someone today for, say, swearing in public or wearing provocative clothing or talking loudly in church. Try objecting to the widespread availability of pornography, or try engaging in non-violent protests outside an abortion clinic, or try explaining to a homosexual friend that his or her lifestyle is unnatural and that he or she will never find true fulfillment, peace, or healing but through Jesus Christ.

Nine times out of 10, the end result of these attempts to "admonish sinners," no matter how gently and compassionately they are performed, is that one is branded an intolerant bigot. After all, what could be a worse, what could be a more politically incorrect attitude in an I'm-OK-you're-OK culture than to tell others, "You're not OK: you're harming yourself and others, at least spiritually and psychologically, if not also physically and sociologically?

The problem is that we live in a society dominated by people who have not made any real psychological or moral progress since they reached adolescence. Thus, they stumble through life with an adolescent understanding of love. To be "loved," to them, means to be affirmed in everything they want to do that does not cause anyone else (except unborn children, the chronically ill, and elderly) grievous bodily harm. Imagine telling someone like that, "Hey, I think you are doing something wrong; I think what you are doing can lead to your spiritual self-destruction and, perhaps, to the spiritual destruction of others, too." They'll likely complain that you are practicing intolerance and bigotry. Yet, it is to spiritually adolescent people like this — to a whole society dominated by such people — that we are called to "speak the truth in love," as St. Paul put it (see Eph 4:15), with both courage and compassion.

It is certainly not easy to do. It takes the virtue of prudence as well: finding just the right moment and just the right words, and saying them in a way that clearly affirms the human dignity of the person you are admonishing, even as they challenge him or her to fulfill his or her highest potential.

Saint Faustina set an excellent example for us in this regard. In her convent in Poland she sometimes discerned the call of the Holy Spirit to practice such "tough love." She actually became known in her religious community for her boldness in admonishing even older and more educated sisters in religion for their sins of malicious gossip, and some of them, in the end, grudgingly respected her for it.

9.2.2. Instruct the Uninformed

This means, first of all, accepting our God-given responsibility to be the primary source of religious education and formation for our children. Some Catholics may be surprised to learn that it is not the local Catholic school upon whom this responsibility primarily rests. Rather, it is the parents.

The *Catechism of the Catholic Church* states that "parents have the first responsibility for the education of their children" (2223), and parents are told that through the grace of matrimony, they "receive the responsibility and privilege of evangelizing their children" (2225). This includes, from an early age, reading to our children and grandchildren Bible stories and stories of the lives of the saints, as well as great Christian works such as *The Chronicles of Narnia*. It means providing them with a steady diet of good Christian CDs and videos and weeding out all the dubious ones from our collection that can only cause the loss of their innocence and the confusion of their developing moral characters.

It means tight restrictions on the cultural rot flowing into our homes through the TV set ("The Devil's tabernacle," as Mother Angelica once called it) and the Internet. It means praying together as a family, too — perhaps by offering a family Rosary or Chaplet of The Divine Mercy or by reciting as prayers the lyrics of good Christian hymns at bedtime. We do not have to turn our homes into monasteries and convents, but we do have to heed the exhortation of St. Paul: "Do not be conformed to this world, be transformed by the renewal of your mind" (Rom 12:2). Beyond our homes, of course, the need for instruction in the true faith is equally urgent. Often there is no more effective (and no less threatening) way to share the Catholic faith with our non-Catholic friends than to do so *in the natural course of friendship itself.* For Christmasses or birthdays, why not give your friends or family members a favorite Catholic book that clearly explains the faith? Most non-Catholics (and non-practicing Catholics) are so full of misinformation about what the Church actually teaches and about the role of the Church down through history that even if a good book given away does no more than break down a few of the prejudices they may hold about Catholicism, then count it as a work of mercy well done.

Try one of these books as gift ideas (all in print at the moment): *Fundamentals of the Faith*, by Peter Kreeft; *Theology for Beginners*, by F.J. Sheed; *Catholic and Christian*, by Alan Shreck (a book that is especially good to share with Evangelical Protestant friends); *Orthodoxy*, by G.K. Chesterton; or *Mere Christianity*, by C.S. Lewis. Finally, read the books yourself first. As St. Peter taught us, "Always be prepared to make a defense to anyone who calls you to account for the hope that is in you, yet do it with gentleness and reverence" (1 Pet 3:15).

9.2.3. Counsel the Doubtful and Comfort the Sorrowful

What a tremendous gift it is from The Divine Mercy when you find someone who really listens to you, who really lets you pour out your heart and share your troubles and miseries, and who then really takes your whole situation in prayer to the Lord *before* presuming to dole out advice to you. Plenty of people are quick to give out half-baked, ill-considered advice! But how many people do you know who *really* listen to you and to the Holy Spirit before they speak?

You can become that person for others if you learn to really listen to the Holy Spirit in your own life first with the help of a spiritual director. Read the New Testament every day and listen to the Lord speaking to you there. Find a good spiritual director and listen to the Lord speaking to you through his or her wise counsel. Then, having learned to listen, you will be ready and able to listen deeply to others.

We can find a good example of this in the life of St. Faustina. In her religious community, she was apparently such a good listener she earned the nickname "the dump" from her fellow sisters because they were always dumping their problems on her (see her *Diary*, 871). It's not hard to discover from her *Diary* where she learned this art of listening. She learned it from listening to the Holy Spirit in prayer and from the same Spirit speaking to her through the guidance of her spiritual directors, such as Fr. Joseph Andrasz, S.J., and Blessed Michael Sopocko.

9.2.4. Be Patient With Those in Error

This is a tough one. In God's merciful love, we certainly ought to share the Catholic Faith with those who are far from Him because they need His mercy so badly. (Don't we all!) It is an act of merciful love to share the faith with those who need it and to pray for them. On the other hand, we must be patient with God's work in other people's lives. We must never harass, pressure, or manipulate anyone. There is a famous bumper sticker that reads, "Please be patient: God is not finished with me yet!" That sums up pretty well what our attitude should be. Our job is but to sow the seeds of faith in the hearts and minds of those who are in grievous error. But change has to come in God's own time. Even if we never see for ourselves the fruit of our efforts, God will surely do His part to water with the grace of conversion the seeds we have planted, when and if people are ready to receive that gift. Until then, we are just to be patient with those in error, to share the truth with them as best we can (acknowledging all the while our own limited grasp of God's revealed truth and limited capacity to adequately express that truth to others), and to pray for them, trusting in God's mercy and patience with us all.

9.2.5. Forgive Offenses

"'Vengeance is mine, I will repay,' says the Lord" (Rom 12:19). If there is any vengeance that needs to be "dished out," in this life or the next, the only One qualified to do it is the Lord, for He alone knows the secrets of all hearts. Thus, we must always let go of any desire in our hearts for vengeance, and in that sense at least, to forgive our enemies. That means stopping ourselves from exacting "petty vengeance" as well, which includes the use of detraction or slander or gossip to get back at people for the evil they may have done to us. In short, we are not to curse the darkness, but to pray for those in darkness. (See Mt 5:44.) Whatever temporal harm they may have done to us, those who are evil are in danger of the greatest harm of all: everlasting loss and condemnation. What they have caused us to suffer pales in comparison to what they will suffer eternally if they do not repent.

However, forgiveness is probably the most misunderstood of all the works of mercy. It does NOT mean blindly letting oneself be victimized. You have a duty to protect yourself and your loved ones from harm, for you are all children of God whom He made in His own image and for whom He gave His life on the Cross. That's how valuable and precious you are in the eyes of our merciful Savior! Forgiving our enemies, therefore, is entirely compatible with reasonable acts of self-protection. For example, forgiveness is entirely compatible with having criminals arrested and placed behind bars where they cannot do further harm to the innocent. Forgiveness is even compatible with the use of legal force by the police or the military, as a last resort, in fending off violent criminals or aggressive foreign powers. (See Catechism, 2263-2267.)

Clearly, the duty to forgive your enemies is compatible with protecting yourself and your loved ones from harm and demanding high standards of conduct from those close to you, including your own close family members. To prevent and block the spread of evil in these ways is actually a work of mercy, not only toward yourself and your loved ones, but even toward the perpetrators of evil. The perpetrators, after all, often have little chance of ever coming to repentance without the help of the "reality therapy" meted out by those charged with the social responsibility of defending the innocent. In other words, to love and forgive your enemies is not necessarily to let them trample all over you. When there is no effective way to defend oneself or others from harm, then that may be the time and the place meekly to carry the cross of persecution. But that time and place is certainly not *every* time and *every* place!

9.2.6. Pray for the Living and the Dead

Every day we are to bring our needs, the needs of our loved ones, and the needs of the whole world into the merciful Heart of Jesus. Saint Faustina herself often did this, bringing them into Christ's "most compassionate Heart" (see *Diary*, 1209-1229).

Our works of mercy, both corporal and spiritual, will always appear inadequate compared to the needs of the world around us. But our Lord does not ask us to meet every need. We are only asked to do what we can and leave the rest to Him as He works out His loving plan for each human soul. Remember the "five loaves and two fish principle." Saint Andrew said to Jesus, "There is a lad here who has five barley loaves and two fish; but what are they among so many?" (Jn 6:9). That meager supply, when offered in faith to Jesus, was found to be enough to feed multitudes. So will our seemingly meager efforts to practice the corporal and spiritual works of mercy, guided by His Spirit and offered up to Jesus. He can work miracles with such little offerings. Some of those miracles we will never even see with our own eyes until we meet Him face-to-face in heaven. It is then when He will give us the grace to see what He sees; it is then when He will turn His loving gaze upon us and we will hear those blessed words from His own lips: "Well done, good and faithful servant!" (Mt 25:23).

9.3. An Exhortation of St. Theresa of Avila

Christ has no body on earth now but yours, no hands but yours, no feet but yours. Yours are the eyes through which the compassion of Christ must look out on the world. Yours are the feet with which He is to go about doing good. Yours are the hands with which He is to bless His people.

CHAPTER TEN

THE PERIL OF FALSE MERCY

It was and is the will of Our Lord Jesus Christ that all who come to Him with faith and repentance receive the Mercy and forgiveness of God, and He won these great gifts for all mankind by His most bloody death on the Cross. But He established a prerequisite for every man, woman, or child who would come to Him, to receive these gifts: namely, faith and penance. It was with this exhortation, that He began His public ministry, when He said, *"The time is accomplished, and the kingdom of God is at hand: repent, and believe the gospel. "* (Mk 1:15) **These words are both an exhortation unto the end of time and the very form and practice of our Holy Religion.**

10.1. The Path of true Repentance & Faith which Christ taught

When a man recognizes that he is a sinner, he comes to Christ by confessing his sins and professing His faith in the Lord Jesus, as God and his Redeemer. He accepts Christ's teaching as a whole, that is entirely and in every respect, and he submits to the authority of Christ which He handed down, in part, to the Apostles and through them to all the Bishops and priests of His Church. To be incorporated into Christ, therefore, a sinner must present himself to a Catholic priest and receive Baptism, making a profession of faith in Christ and His teachings, and repenting of all his sins. **He shows publicly that he is sincere in his repentance by removing himself from the public profession of sin, which consists in those forms or lifestyles which are contrary to the Gospel.** Thus, drunkards give up drink and remove it from their homes; fornicators give up fornication, adulterers leave their lovers, sodomites give up their sodomy and its lifestyle, etc.

For Catholics, who have fallen away from the practice of the Faith, and have entered into sinful relations, such as marrying one who is already married but separated or divorced, or cohabiting with anyone, **the return to the practice of the Faith requires this same repentance and faith, separation from the life of sin and reception of the Sacrament of Confession. Then one can receive the Eucharist.** In the Catholic Church, we take the Sacraments seriously, because we believe just as Our Lord taught us, that in the Eucharist there is really, truly and substantially the Body and Blood, Soul and Divinity of the Most High and Holy

God of Israel, the Eternal Son of God, Jesus Christ, before whom, even in Christ, no one is worthy to come, unless he repent and believe, but by Whose mercy and grace a man is made worthy to receive in the Sacrament of the Eucharist, if he repent of his sins and believe the entirety (not just what he picks and chooses) of the Gospel.

This is the discipline and faith which the Catholic Church has received from Our Lord Himself, through the Apostles, and from the Apostles through the very men they chose for Bishops and priests (presbyters), and through these down through the ages. Our teachings and disciplines have never changed, because they are not ours, but Christ's, and our Church, the Catholic Church is not ours, but Christ's. The Catholic Church, therefore, being the one of which Christ said: *And I say to you: That you are Peter; and upon this rock I will build My Church, and the gates of Hell shall not prevail against her. (Matthew 16:18)*, knows that this Faith which Christ gave her is her victory over the world, the flesh and Satan; to alter that Faith therefore, would be to succumb to the world, the flesh and Satan. This is what we have always believed, this is what Christ and the Apostles have taught, and not only to us, but to all the world.

For it is mercy to preach repentance to sinners, as Our Lord commanded St. Peter and the Apostles, when He ascended into Heaven. It is false mercy to preach acceptance of sinners without repentance and faith, since that leaves them in the state of sin in which they merit eternal damnation and temporal punishments.

False Mercy is by simple definition the contrary of Divine Mercy and Divine Mercy is love acting for us, Divine love from the offended which is God to the transgressors which is us, so... False mercy is just that, action build to deceive. False is something that is not true, something that doesn't hold at all, is something that looks, sounds, feels or smells real but at the same time is not. When falseness combines with Mercy the definition becomes a little broader, it is a set of things, because Mercy is one thing us humans seek to heal our souls, to silence or guilt and reach out to God to welcome us back, something we need to feel at peace, it is the Light of God and without we are in darkness.

Darkness today feels normal, the world is entirely in darkness, it is run by darkness, but our souls are made in God's image and what belongs to God needs God, so when Mercy is preached immediately creates in us the spiritual urge to embrace it, as we are spiritual beings, but we are blinded by the world and by our very flesh, so False Mercy becomes attractive when we hear what our flesh wants to hear. "...For this I was born and for this I came into the world, to testify to the truth. Everyone who belongs to the truth listens to my voice." John 18:37. Seeing sin as nothing, that we are all save, all of this, without true repentance is False Mercy.

Many are helping false Mercy with the "respect" card, by not saying the truth, those who don't say the truth are harming those who belong to God, by not knowing the truth they stay in sin and after death, sin with no repentance, can open the doors of hell; truth will set you free (John 8:32) said the Lord, because total truth will make you want to rethink, you either embrace the truth and repent (John 18:37) or you'll reject truth and continue in your sin.

False Mercy has the whole world and the devil protecting it with a call of bigotry, lack of understanding, sometimes calling people haters and legalists, even if you are denouncing the wicked acts, not who commits them, they say that you are judging people, when you are proclaiming the Gospel, because you are only repeating what God says and the world don't like it, hate for those who proclaim the truth. "If the world hates you, realize that it hated me first. If you belonged to the world, the world would love its own; but because you do not belong to the world, and I have chosen you out of the world, the world hates you. John 15:18-19

But the world needs those who proclaim the Gospel to become corrupt and preach false Mercy, so many souls relax about seeking perfection and because the flesh has the urge to sin and you can't control yourself, then you sin, but with false Mercy is alright, because God "understands"... God doesn't give a law to then ignore His own law **don't be deceive**. People want to embrace false Mercy because it gives you what your flesh needs, it calms your conscience with exactly what you want to hear, not what your soul truly needs, this is why many embrace strange teachings and many pastors are happy to give it, because they are blinded themselves out of their own sin, sin they believe don't exist or believe that God "understands" and forgives you automatically.

False Mercy is on the outside beautiful and attractive, way too easy and way too mundane... Loving the Lord is hard, following His commandments only creates enemies and pure hate from those you use to love or those who come to know you, despite that, follow the Lord and don't despair, don't hold a grudge... continue to love truth and trust the Lord. Reject False Mercy, reject darkness, reject the devil and his works, many will say he doesn't exist but he does, and many will fight to protect him even un-knowingly FIGHT, fight, fight... your Lord Jesus is with you, nothing will harm you, even those who claim to be His apostles, preachers of falseness, look at their fruits, their bad fruits and you'll know them, false prophets (Mat 7:15-16) reject darkness, may the Lord give us the grace to repent and love Him perfectly in truth.

10.2. Mercy is False when it Opposes the Righteousness of God

But is there no mercy for the penitent? Certainly there is. In repentance there is no encouragement to evil; on the contrary, in it evil is condemned. Faith in Christ is the perfection of repentance since therein only can we be effectually delivered from sin. Repentance must be genuine. Mercy without repentance for sins is used for this end; it appears to be nothing else than a complacent look on the sinner and his sins.

It is necessary to discern between this one-sided mercy and true mercy which fully invites to conversion, to the rejection of sin. True mercy, which implies this initial, extremely touching movement of God toward the sinner and His misery, continues in a moment of the creature's conversion to God: "God desires not the death of the wicked, but that the wicked turn from his way and live" (cf. Ezek 33:11). **Hence the Gospels insist on the duty of conversion, renunciation and penance.** *Our Lord went so far as to say: "Unless you do penance, you shall all perish" (cf. Lk 13:5). This call to conversion is the heart of the Gospel, which we find in St. John the Baptist as well as in St. Peter. When sinners, touched by preaching, ask what they must do, they hear only this recommendation: "be converted and do penance."*

Now the new preachers of a new mercy insist so much on the first step taken by God toward human beings who are lost because of sin, ignorance and misery that they too often omit this second movement, which must come from the creature: repentance, conversion, the rejection of sin. Ultimately, the new mercy is nothing but complacency about sin. God loves you... no matter what.

10.3. New Mercy with no Repentance

A Latin word that we encounter so often and that obviously must be on our lips is "*Miserere*." This word indicates, for our part, the acknowledgment of our misery, and then our appeal to God's mercy. The awareness of our misery makes us ask for forgiveness, fills us with contrition and is accompanied by the intention not to sin again. The true love that inspires this movement causes us to understand the necessity of making reparation for our sins. Hence the expiatory sacrifice is satisfactory.

These various movements are necessary for the conversion that obtains the forgiveness of the God of mercy, who—in truth—does not want the death of the sinner but that he be converted and live. The claim to eternal happiness is completely illusory in someone who is unwilling to break with his sinful habits and does not seriously want to flee the occasions of sin or to make a resolution not to start sinning again.

Preaching a sort of mercy without the necessary conversion of poor sinners would be a message devoid of meaning for heaven, a diabolical trap that would tranquilize the world in its folly and its increasingly open rebellion against God, whereas heaven is quite positive about it: "God is not mocked" (Gal 6:7).

The lives of human beings in the world today are calling down the wrath of God on every side. The massacre of innocent children in their mother's wombs, by the millions, the legalization of unnatural unions, and euthanasia are crimes that cry out to Heaven, not to mention all sorts of injustices….

10.4. MERCY QUOTES

Mercy: "Relief of distress or compassion shown to victims of misfortune.
A blessing that is an act of Divine compassion." **-Noah Webster (1758 - 1843)**

"Open thy gates of mercy, gracious God!
My soul flies through these wounds to seek out thee."
-William Shakespeare (1564 - 1616)

"Grace is getting what we do not deserve.
Mercy is not receiving what we do deserve."
Our Daily Bread (July 12, 1998)

"All great things are simple, and many can be expressed in single words:
freedom, justice, honor, duty, mercy, hope."
-Sir Winston Churchill (1874 - 1965)

"With the merciful You will show Yourself merciful."
-Psalm 18:25
"I would say to my soul, O my soul, this is not the place of despair; this is not the time to despair in. As long as mine eyes can find a promise in the Bible, as long as there is a moment left me of breath or life in this world, so long will I wait or look for mercy, so long will I fight against unbelief and despair."
-John Bunyan (1628 - 1688)

"Among the attributes of God, although they are all equal,
mercy shines with even more brilliancy than justice."
-Miguel De Cervantes (1547 - 1616)

"God's mercy is boundless, free and, through Jesus Christ our Lord,
available to us now in our present situation."
-A.W. Tozer (1897 - 1963)

"The mercy of God is the loadstone to draw sinners to him."
T. Watson, A Body of Divinity

"The pearl of justice is found in the heart of mercy."
-Catherine of Siena (1347 - 1380)

"Mercy is God substituting his favor for his wrath."
-Rev. D. Sadler

"We shall only resist social injustice and the disintegration of community if justice and mercy prevail in our own common life and social differences have lost their power to divide."
-Hendrik Berkhof

He giveth more grace when the burdens grow greater, He sendeth more strength when the labors increase; To added affliction he addeth his mercy, To multiplied trials, His multiplied peace.
-Annie Johnson Flint (1862-1932)

"Surely goodness and mercy will follow me all the days of my life."
-King David

Teach me to feel another's woe, To hide the fault I see; That mercy I to others show, That mercy show to me. **-Alexander Pope (1688-1744)**

"Nothing is ever lost by courtesy. It is the cheapest of the pleasures; costs nothing and conveys much. It pleases him who gives and him who receives, and thus, like mercy, it is twice blessed."
-Erastus Wiman

Shall I doubt my Father's mercy? Shall I think of death as doom,
Or the stepping o'er the threshold To a bigger, brighter room?
-Robert Freeman (1878-1940)
"He who demands mercy and shows none burns
the bridges over which he himself must later pass."
-Thomas Adams (1612-1653)

"God's Grace is immeasurable; His mercy inexhaustible;
His peace inexpressible." **–Unknown**

"We do pray for mercy; And that same prayer doth teach us all to render the deeds of mercy."
-William Shakespeare (1564-1616)

"Trust the past to the mercy of God, the present
to his love, and the future to his providence."
-Saint Augustine of Hippo (354-430)

"Our prayer and God's mercy are like two buckets in a well;
while the one ascends the other descends."
-Mark Hopkins (1802-1887)

The quality of mercy is not strain'd, it droppeth as the gentle rain from heaven
Upon the place beneath: it is twice blest; it blesseth him that gives and him that takes.
-Shakespeare, The Merchant of Venice, act 4, scene 1.

"God gave to sinful mankind the greatest gift of mercy when He sent
His only begotten Son Yeshua to the Cross on our behalf."
- Rabbi Mike Short

"I will trust in the mercy of God forever and ever."
- Paslm 52:8.

"We were all in the human condition before we were born again of God.
Remember that and have the God kind of mercy for others in the human condition."
- Rev. Barbara Di Gilio

"Mercy is exercised only where there is guilt. It always pre-supposes guilt.
The penalty of the law must have been previously incurred,
else there can be no scope for mercy."
Charles G. Finney (May 7, 1845)

Give to everyone who asks you, for truly this is the way that God loves to give.
St. Clement of Alexandria

Be merciful in order that you might receive mercy. **Bishop St. Polycarp, Epistle
2.3**

Be merciful as our heavenly Father is merciful. **Jesus in Luke 6:36**
Blessed are the merciful for they will be shown mercy. **Matthew 5:7**

"The unfailing love of the Lord never ends!
By his mercies we have been kept from complete destruction.
Great is His faithfulness; His mercies begin afresh each new day."
-Jeremiah, the prophet

"God's justice condemns us--but His mercy redeems us"
Our Daily Bread (August 22, 1995)

"God's wisdom is manifold because God is inexhaustible in His wonder, and in His
mercy." **--John Adam Woods**

"Return, O LORD, deliver my soul: oh save me for Thy mercies' sake."
--Psalms 6:4

"To those who love God's mercy, nothing 'unredeemable' can happen to you!"
-Unknown

CONCLUSION

Let us take this appeal to mercy seriously, as the inhabitants of Nineveh did! Let us go in search of the lost sheep, let us pray for the conversion of souls, let us perform as much as we can all the works of mercy, both material and especially the spiritual works, for there is a serious shortage of the latter. *We must ask the God of mercy for an ever deeper conversion to holiness and implore the graces and pardons of His infinite mercy.*

Fortunately, there's *always, always, always* a way out, this side of eternity. If you're not in the spiritual state you need to be, there's an easy cure. Repent, go to confession, gets washed clean in the Blood of Christ, and receive that *outpouring* of graces. Choose Christ at all costs, choose Christ over all earthly loves and pleasures, and do whatever it takes to be able to receive Him wholly and completely, Body and Blood, Soul and Divinity. When you do that, you'll know what true mercy feels like.

As we know from Scripture, Tradition, liturgy, and the lives of the saints, God's mercy is quite different. He demands conversion, repentance, abandoning the sin, embarking on the hard road of virtue, embracing the Cross—and doing this as many times as it takes, stumbling, falling, and yet getting up again, until God is truly the One loved above all things and in all things. His is a mercy that heals by cauterizing the wound, removing debris, resetting broken bones, taking away self-indulgences that are fatal to us: it is, in the famous phrase, a severe mercy. God's mercy is bound up in His penetrating judgment of our souls,

We will never be vessels and ambassadors of mercy to the world unless we act from a right understanding and acceptance of *God's* strong and demanding mercy towards *us*. When Christian leaders alter the truth of sin, they actually block the way for sinners like us to know Mercy. Such 'mercy' is a misnomer and as cruel as death. It could cost souls eternal life. The cost is higher for the blind guides. They put a huge stumbling block in the way of God's little ones, incurring a judgment described by Jesus as 'drowning by millstone around neck.' (Lk. 17:2).

Jesus warns us all: 'So watch yourselves.' (v.3) Kindness without truth is false Mercy. It appeals to our delusion that we can have Heaven and our lusts too. Wake up. Peter woke up his flock with this warning about false prophets: 'By appealing to the lustful desires of sinful human nature, they entice people who are just escaping from those who live in error. They promise them freedom while they themselves are slaves of depravity.' (2P2:18, 19)

No truth, no Mercy. In my early days of repentance, I knew one thing for sure. Jesus calls us to die. Mercy oils our surrender; Mercy fills the empty, lonely soul and raises him up. *'Woe to those who call evil good and good evil, who put darkness for light and light for darkness…' (Is. 5:20, 21)*

'Father, grant us clarity as to what pleases You and what does not. Thank you for the clear witness of Scripture and the Church. Help us to discern 'blind guides'; most importantly, help us to discern our own tendency to conform the truth to our lusts. We especially pray for Christians caught in lies of their own design. Set them free before it is too late. Let the truth set us free for Mercy.'

BOOK DESCRIPTION

The Book, *"Rich in Mercy: Experiencing and Practicing the Mercy of God"* is written as a resource for Christians to meditate more deeply on how to experience God's Mercy and at the same as a tool to encourage them to practice Mercy and be merciful as our heavenly Father is merciful. Fr. Dr. Constant Leke shows how God takes steps towards human beings who are lost because of sin, ignorance and misery. He also goes further to urge sinners who wish to experience God's mercy of the need of repentance, conversion and the rejection of sin. The book calls all to reject a one-sided mercy and live by mercy in all its aspects. Moreover, he urges all to take advantage of the call of the Gospel to ask the God of mercy for an ever deeper conversion to holiness and implore the graces and pardons of God's mercy. Lastly, the book has a clear message of warning Christians of the perils and danger of false mercy which can easily lead to the pathways of Hell. Anyone who reads through the book will surely experiencing the restoring mercy of God and will be shown in what ways a Christian can practice true mercy.

ABOUT THE AUTHOR

Rev. Fr. Dr. Constant Leke is a Catholic Priest of the Diocese of Mamfe-Cameroon. He was ordained on the 27th of April 2011. He spent 9 years (2013-2022) working in the Sankt Mariae Rosenkranz Parish, Mulheim- Diocese of Essen-Germany. He has Doctorate Degree in New Testament Studies from the Ruhr University, Bochum-Germany.

Printed by Books on Demand GmbH, Norderstedt / Germany